Becoming a Better
COMMUNICATOR

A Basic Course in Interpersonal and Public Communication

Workbook

Third Edition
Revised Printing

Denise J. Miller
Oral Roberts University

required to accompany the textbook

Kendall Hunt
publishing company

First edition self-published by the author.

Upper left cover photo: PeopleImages/Getty Images
All other cover images: © Shutterstock

www.kendallhunt.com
Send all inquiries to:
4050 Westmark Drive
Dubuque, IA 52004-1840

Student name _____

Semester (Fall, Spring, or Summer) _____Year_____Section #_____

Professor's name _____

Professor's contact information _____

Professor's office hours _____

General notes for the course _____

_____

Scripture or biblical principle for the course _____

_____

_____

Personal goal for the semester _____

_____

_____

*Special thanks to Carole Lewandowski, Professor Emeritus and
all the faculty and students who have contributed to the classes and
curriculum of Oral Communication at Oral Roberts University*

Table of Contents

Grades: Tools and Tips

Grade Computation

Graded Item	Student's Score	Value	Total Points	Possible
UNIT EXAMS				
EXAM I_____+ obj_____+ vocab_____		X2		200
EXAM II_____+ obj_____+ vocab_____		X2		200
EXAM III_____+ obj_____+ vocab_____		X2		200
GROUP PROJECT				
Individual Grade		X1		100
Presentation Grade		X1		100
INFORMATIVE SPEECH				
Outline		X1.5		150
Oral Presentation		X1.5		150
PERSUASIVE SPEECH				
Outline		X2		200
Oral Presentation		X2		200
OTHER				
Home/classwork		X1		100
Reflections		X1		200
Final Exam		X2		200 (Summer 0)
SUBTOTAL				2000 (Summer 1800)
EXTRA CREDIT (other than attendance)				
ATTENDANCE				67 (Summer 60)
Absences _____ Tardies _____ 3 tardies = 1 absence	Abs adjusted for tardies: _____-	# of abs allowed: _____=	# of EXCESSIVE absences: _____	*Attendance Score*

Add 3.3% (67 points) (60 summer) for perfect attendance.
Subtract a letter grade (200) (180 summer) for each excessive absence.

Fall and Spring	Summer
1800 – 2000 = A	1530 – 1700 = A
1600 – 1799 = B	1360 – 1529 = B
1400 – 1599 = C	1190 – 1359 = C
1200 – 1399 = D	1020 – 1189 = D

FINAL GRADE:

Extra Credit

I. Achieve **perfect attendance** for **67 points** (60 points for summer).
   A. Arrive on time and remain until the class is dismissed.
   B. Come to every class unless you have an administrative excuse.

II. Submit appropriate paperwork for **seminars or dramas** for **5 points** each or elimination of **excessive absences** (2 seminars/dramas = 1 absence).
   A. Find instructions in this workbook p. _____
   B. Submit the **handwritten** paperwork at the beginning of the next class meeting after the event.
      1. Dramas outside this university are eligible for extra credit by faculty approval if one drama from this university is also submitted.
      2. Seminars outside of this university are eligible for extra credit by faculty approval and if one seminar from this university is also submitted.
      3. Partial credit is not available for dramas and/or seminars.

III. Handwrite **vocabulary definitions** from the textbook **and responses to the objectives** from the workbook for each of the chapters of a unit exam for up to **60 points.**
   A. Choose the vocabulary or the objectives, or both for any or all of the 3 unit exams.
      1. Add 1% per chapter to your exam score for **handwriting** the responses to all of the workbook objectives for each chapter tested except obj. A.
      2. Add 1% per chapter to your exam score for **handwriting** all of the vocabulary and their definitions for each of the chapters of an exam.
      3. Add 2% per chapter to your exam score for **handwriting** all the objectives and vocabulary for each of the chapters of an exam.
   B. Be neat and timely. (Partial credit is not available for a unit of objectives.)
      1. Start each chapter on a fresh sheet or set of note cards.
      2. Write the labels such as "1B" very plainly.
      3. Turn in the objectives before the exam.
   C. Use either paper or notecards for vocabulary and/or objectives.

There are 2000 points available in this basic communication course.

100 extra credit points = ½ of a letter grade.

Drama and Seminar Extra Credit

Handwritten EXTRA CREDIT is **due at the beginning of the class immediately following the event.**

> **Instructions for the DRAMA:** Practice identifying concepts from the textbook, *Becoming a Better Communicator*.

1. **Handwrite** a full page response and submit it to your professor at the beginning of the next class.
2. Describe examples from the drama that illustrate ten (10) of the textbook vocabulary words.
3. Format your handwritten paper.
   - Include the heading in the upper left margin: student's name, professor's name, section, date.
   - Title the paper: Drama Reflection for Extra Credit, then title of the show and playwright on the top, 2nd and 3rd lines.
   - Highlight the ten terms with color.

    Example: Drama Reflection for Extra Credit
                              Charlotte's Web
                              By E.B. White

When Fern told Wilber she loved him, she used her soft facial expression to **compliment** her words. (Continue with nine more examples of vocabulary words from *Becoming a Better...*)

> **Instructions for the SEMINAR:** Practice active listening.

1. **Handwrite** a full page response and submit it to your professor at the beginning of our class immediately following the event.
2. Copy and answer these five questions with full sentences.
   - What was your favorite part of the seminar?
   - In what way could you relate to the topic?
   - What did you learn?
   - What did you like or dislike about the ending of the seminar?
   - What questions were left unanswered?
3. Format your handwritten paper.
   - Include the heading in the upper left margin: student's name, professor's name, section, date.
   - Title the paper: Seminar Reflection for Extra Credit, then title of the seminar and the presenter's name on the top, 2nd and 3rd lines.
   - Highlight the 5 questions with color.

    Example: Seminar Reflection for Extra Credit
                              "Innovators Rule"
                              By Pat Cain

What was your favorite part of the seminar? My favorite part of the seminar included... (Continue answering this question. Then write the next four questions and answers.)

Ace the Course

I. **Gather materials.**
    - Scantron(s) for exams (depending on the professor)
    - Syllabus (online)
    - Calendar (electronic or paper)
    - Video recording equipment such as a smart phone
    - Textbook and **new, current** workbook.

II. **Exchange contact information.**
    - To work with classmates on assignments and exam reviews
    - To ask classmates to turn in assignments, and get information for missed classes

III. **Set electronic alerts using the syllabus calendar.**
    - For reviewing and taking exams
        - Imagine application questions for objectives and vocabulary
        - Review with online PowerPoints
    - For presentations
        - Schedule research, interviewing, and outlining
        - Prepare visuals and practice aloud

IV. **Read each chapter.**
    - Read the chapter summary, discussion questions and headings first.
    - HANDWRITE responses to the workbook objectives and/or vocabulary for **extra credit** as you read.
    - Draw models and diagrams to improve comprehension and memory.
    - Re-read the summary.

V. **Use class time.**
    - Participate.
        - Ask and answer questions.
        - Volunteer.
        - Avoid distractions.
    - Earn **extra credit** for perfect attendance, always on time, staying the entire period.

Adaptive Course Calendar

Week	Date	Class Topic	Due at the Beginning of Class
1		Class Orientation, Better Communicator's Overview *Optional: Assignment of:* • *Self-Introduction Speech in workbook* • *Annotated Bibliography in workbook* • *Orientation Quiz*	Chapter 1
2		Self-Aware, Perceptive, *Optional:* • *Fish Philosophy* • *Johari Window(assigned one day for home-work, analyzed another day)* • *YouTube Perception Check 101* • *Chapter quizzes*	Chapters 2 and 3
3		Nonverbal Assign Group Project pages in workbook • *Presentation rubric* • *Interpersonal rubric* • *Reflection* *Optional:* • *Nonverbal Hunt* • *Group officers/norm setting from workbook* • *Exam Review Preparation in workbook* • *Chapter Quiz*	Chapter 4
4		Listening Assign Interpersonal Reflection Exam I *Optional:* • *Exam Review from workbook* • *Role playing non-empathic listening* • *Chapter Quiz*	Chapters 5 Exam I: Ch. 1, 2, 3, 4, 5
5		Connected, Diverse, Aware of Words *Optional:* • *Hofstede's Country Comparison* • *YouTube Key and Peele's code switching "Phone Call"* • *YouTube Joy Luck Club "Meet the Parents"*	Chapters 6, 7, 8

		• *Group Problem-solving simulation with data collection and interpretation in class* • *"Resisting Manipulation" role playing by Terry Gillen* • *"Say 'No' Gracefully" by Christine Carter* • *Chapter Quizzes*	
6		Group 1 and 2 Presentations: Problem Solvers Group 3 and 4 Presentations: Leaders and Followers *Optional:* • *Practice I – You statements in Ch. 9 sidebar* • *Practice the 4-step apology in Ch. 9 sidebar*	Group Presentations Chapters 9 and 10
7		Exam II Assign Interview Homework pages from Workbook Considerate *Optional:* • *Roleplay interview CAR from Workbook* • *Assign audience analysis from Workbook*	Exam II: Ch. 6, 7, 8, 9, 10 Chapter 11 Corporate Reflection of the Group Project with personal paragraph Completed peer grading for Interpersonal Communication in Group Settings, 4B
8		Informative, Organized *Optional:* • *mid-term course evaluation* • *Informative Speech Outline Workshop I*	Chapters 12, 13
9		Confident Begin Informative Speech Presentations *Optional:* • *Informative Speech Outline Workshop 2* • *Visuals* • *Virtual Reality app for Presentation Skills* • *Videographer, Timer, Friendly Evaluator*	Chapter 14 Three supports for each main point Informative Speech Presentations
10		Informative Speech Presentations Assign Informative Speech Reflection	Informative Speech Presentations Reflection of Interpersonal Communication
11		Informative Speech Presentations Persuasion	Informative Speech Presentations Chapter 15
12		Persuasive Speech Workshop I Exam III	Reflection of the Informative Speech

			Three supports for each main point of the Persuasive Speech Exam III: Ch. 11, 12, 13, 14, 15, and Appendices A, B, C, D
13		Persuasive Speech Presentations with Question & Answer sessions Assign Reflection of Persuasive Speech	Persuasive Speech Presentations
14		Persuasive Speech Presentations with Question & Answer sessions	Persuasive Speech Presentations
15		Persuasive Speech Presentations with Question & Answer sessions	Persuasive Speech Presentations
16		Student Opinion Survey *Optional:* • *Grade Reconciliation* • *Awards, Eulogies, Toasts*	Professor's choice
Finals		**Final Exam**	**Ch. 1 – 15 Appendices A - D**

All students from all sections:
- Take the final exam together **Monday evening** from 5:30 p.m. until 7:15 p.m.
- Wear dress code.
- Bring a scantron and pencil.
- Bring no food, drink, electronics, bags, books, or phones into the testing area.
- Record days, dates, and chapters for each exam below:

	Day of Week	Month and Day	Chapters (appendices)
Exam I	………………………	…………………………………	Ch. 1-5
Exam II	………………………	…………………………………	Ch. 6-10
Exam III	………………………	…………………………………	Ch. 11-15, Appendices A-D
Final Exam	Monday	…………………………………	Ch. 1-15, Appendices A-D

Reading Objectives: Exam Study Guides

All exam items are multiple choice questions based on the following objectives and the textbook.

- The exam questions come from the textbook and not class lecture because of the multiple sections of the course.
- Many exam items require application of the concepts.
- Some professors award extra credit for handwriting responses to these objectives.
- More information on exams, including dates are in the syllabus.

Chapter 1 Better Communicator's Overview

A. Define all the vocabulary words on the last page of the chapter
B. List and briefly explain the eight principles of communication.
C. Explain the difference between verbal and non-verbal symbols.
D. List and explain the elements of communication.
E. Explain how a person can be both a sender and a receiver at the same time.
F. Explain the difference between encoding and decoding.
G. List and describe the three characteristics of channels.
H. List and describe the three types of interference.
I. List and explain the types of context.
J. List and explain the five types of communicative context.
K. Explain how differing frames of reference can contribute to misunderstanding.
L. Give the ethical implication given in the chapter that seemed most important to you and explain why. You can disagree with one if you wish; just explain why you disagree.

Chapter 2 Better Communicators are Self-aware

A. Define all the vocabulary words on the last page of the chapter.
B. Explain the difference between self-awareness, self-concept and identity.
C. List the things that we use to develop our sense of self.
D. Explain how self-fulfilling prophecy and generalized other relate to reflected appraisal.
E. List and briefly explain the possible reactions to facework.
F. Explain how mass media can be an element of social comparison.
G. Recreate the graphic that shows the Johari Window.
H. Describe the difference between high and low self-monitors.
I. List and briefly explain the levels of emotional intelligence.
J. Give the tips for improving the accuracy of your self-concept.
K. Give the ethical implication given in the chapter that seemed most important to you and explain why. You can disagree with one if you wish; just explain why you disagree.

Chapter 3 Better Communicators are Perceptive

A. Define all the vocabulary words on the last page of the chapter.
B. Give the two characteristics of communication that affect perception.
C. List and briefly describe the three steps in the perceptual process.
D. List and briefly describe three things that affect selection.
E. List and briefly explain the ways we can organize stimuli, based on constructivism.
F. Explain the similarity between closure and perceptual constancy.
G. List some things that influence interpretation.
H. Explain how your filters affect what you can perceive and how you accidentally mislead others.
I. Give an example of a time that you have used ambiguous language to deceive another or another person has used it to deceive you.
J. Give the ethical implication given in the chapter that seemed most important to you and explain why. You can disagree with one if you wish; just explain why you disagree.

Chapter 4 Better Communicators are Aware of Nonverbal Cues

A. Define all the vocabulary words on the last page of the chapter.
B. List the six principles of non-verbal communication.
C. List the eight functions of non-verbal communication.
D. List the behaviors Edesu and Burgoon said people use to non-verbally overpower someone else.
E. Briefly explain workplace harassment.
F. Give and briefly describe the nine forms of non-verbal communication.
G. Give Hall's proxemics areas with distances.
H. Give the four things that contribute to understanding vocalics (paralanguage).
I. List and briefly describe the four types of touch.
J. Give the ethical implication given in the chapter that seemed most important to you and explain why. You can disagree with one if you wish; just explain why you disagree.

Chapter 5 Better Communicators are Good Listeners

A. Define all the vocabulary words on the last page of the chapter.
B. Explain the difference between hearing and listening.
C. List and briefly explain the steps in the listening process.
D. List and briefly explain the four reasons/purposes (as opposed to styles) of listening.
E. Give the tips for improving listening for information.
F. Give the tips for improving empathetic listening.
G. Give the tips for improving listening for judgement.
H. Give the tips for improving listening for fun.
I. List and briefly describe the perceptual and listening barriers.
J. List and briefly explain the two tests that Fisher said we use to determine if we're being told the truth.

K. Give the ethical implication given in the chapter that seemed most important to you and explain why. You can disagree with one if you wish; just explain why you disagree.

Chapter 6 Better Communicators are Connected

A. Define all the vocabulary words on the last page of the chapter.
B. List and explain the characteristics of interpersonal communication.
C. Create a chart with the benefits of self-disclosure on one side and the risks of self-disclosure on the other side.
D. Draw an image that portrays Social Penetration Theory.
E. Explain the difference between depth and breadth.
F. List and briefly describe the nature or characteristics of friendship.
G. Give Hall's friendship rules.
H. List and briefly describe the characteristics of romantic relationships.
I. List Knapp's five stages of relationship development.
J. List Knapp's five stages of relationship dissolution.
K. List Chapman's love languages.
L. Give the tips for maintaining romantic relationships.
M. List and briefly describe the principles of Systems Theory of Family.
N. List and briefly describe the principles of Kantor & Lehr's family communication styles.
O. Give the tips for maintaining family relationships.
P. Explain the difference between control messages and support messages in parenting.
Q. Give the ethical implication given in the chapter that seemed most important to you and explain why. You can disagree with one if you wish; just explain why you disagree.

Chapter 7 Better Communicators are Sensitive to Diversity

A. Define all the vocabulary words on the last page of the chapter.
B. Explain the difference between cross-cultural communication and code-switching.
C. Give some examples of cultural artifacts from your native culture.
D. Briefly explain the Linguistic Relativity Hypothesis.
E. List Hofstede's cultural differences as pairs of opposites.
F. List and briefly describe the problems that can result when cultures collide.
G. List the major ways that male and female communication differ.
H. Create a table showing the differences between report talk and rapport talk with them on opposite sides of the table.
I. List the ethical implications given in the chapter that seemed most important to you and explain why. You can disagree with one if you wish; just explain why you disagree.

Chapter 8 Better Communicators are Attentive to Words

A. Define all the vocabulary words on the last page of the chapter.

B. Draw and describe Ogden and Richard's triangle of meaning using an example that is different from a lamp.
C. Draw Hayakawa's Ladder of Abstraction with labels on each rung, using an example different from "Mrs. Worth".
D. Give an example of an instance when you used ambiguity to be polite.
E. Identify the scholar who wrote that misunderstandings occur when we wrongly assume that other people use words as we do and that to get along we should discover what people mean, not what words mean.
F. List the four properties of words <u>and</u> give an example of a word that has changed its meaning.
G. Explain how the life of Helen Keller demonstrates the Linguistic Relativity Hypothesis.
H. What is the most dangerous thing to do when you feel ashamed according to Brene' Brown?
I. Contrast the concept of doublespeak with the concept of euphemisms.
J. Write a vivid sentence about your hometown. List the method(s) you used to make it vivid: an action verb, a descriptor, a word picture or celebrity-involvement.
K. List three phrases to cut out of your language for the sake of concision, which can contribute to building a sense of salience.
L. List three types of phrases that powertalkers avoid.
M. List three examples of exclusive language along with a more inclusive expression for each.
N. Give the ethical implication given in the chapter that seemed most important to you and explain why. You can disagree with one if you wish; just explain why you disagree.

Chapter 9 Better Communicators are Problem Solvers

A. Define all the vocabulary words on the last page of the chapter.
B. List and briefly explain some sources of conflict.
C. List and briefly describe the three dialectical tensions.
D. List and briefly explain Gottman's Four Horsemen.
E. Describe the benefits of conflict.
F. Recreate Thomas & Killman's graphic of conflict styles.
G. Identify the four steps for a proper apology.
H. Compose three "you" statements that place blame on the listener along with a more personally powerful "I" statement for each of the three "you" statements.
I. List the tips for dealing with others in authority over you.
J. List the things to remember when you have authority.
K. Give the ethical implication given in the chapter that seemed most important to you and explain why. You can disagree with one if you wish; just explain why you disagree.

Chapter 10 Better Communicators Are Group Leaders/Followers

A. Define all the vocabulary words on the last page of the chapter.
B. When things go wrong, a well-functioning group will avoid blaming individuals. What does the high-functioning group focus on when things go wrong?

C. List and briefly describe the four stages of group development.
D. Describe what leaders can do when people start reacting before they have listened.
E. What does an "Interviewer" need from a leader and how often do you, personally fall into the "interviewer" category?
F. What does a "Bull in a China Shop" need from a leader and how often do you, personally fall into the "Bull in a China Shop" category?
G. What does a "Turtle" need from a leader and how often do you, personally fall into the "Turtle" category?
H. What does an "Ideal" need from a leader and how often do you, personally fall into the "ideal" category?
I. Name a person that you would include in your "Wisdom Tour" and describe why.
J. List two of Charles Duhigg's eight skills of good leadership that you see in yourself.
K. Give an example of a situation in which authoritarian leadership or laissez-faire leadership was more appropriate than a democratic style.
L. When does a situational leader shift from being a directing leader to a coaching leader?
M. When does the situational leader move from the supporting phase into the delegating phase?
N. What method/skill does a servant leader use when she prefers to cultivate a solution rather than create a solution?
O. Give an example of a servant leader embracing his follower's weaknesses and strengths.
P. Describe something you or someone that you know has done that "built community".
Q. When your information is contrary to what the group seems to want to hear, what can you add to your statements to increase the chance that the group will consider your information?
R. Describe two of the eight behaviors that may indicate that the helpful quality of group cohesion is shifting into the destructive quality of Groupthink.
S. List two of the five safeguards leaders (you) may use to avoid Groupthink.
T. Give the ethical implication given in the chapter that seemed most important to you and explain why. You can disagree with one if you wish; just explain why you disagree.

Chapter 11 Better Communicators Are Considerate

A. Define all the vocabulary words on the last page of the chapter.
B. List and briefly explain four ways our perceptions can cause us to be wrong.
C. List and briefly explain the attribution errors.
D. List and briefly explain the demographic items you must consider when analyzing an audience.
E. List and briefly explain the things you must consider when analyzing an occasion.
F. Give the questions you should ask yourself when picking your topic.
G. Give the ethical implication given in the chapter that seemed most important to you and explain why. You can disagree with one if you wish; just explain why you disagree.

Chapter 12 Better Communicators are Informative

A. Define all the vocabulary words on the last page of the chapter.

B. List four things a speech topic should be.
C. Explain how being focused on serving the audience helps the speaker's speech anxiety.
D. List and briefly describe the types of informative speeches.
E. List and briefly describe the types of general speech purposes.
F. List and briefly explain three things you should keep in mind when researching a speech.
G. List information sources for informative speeches.
H. Give some tips for conducting for an informational interview.
I. Explain the differences between neutral, leading, and loaded questions.
J. Give the ethical implication given in the chapter that seemed most important to you and explain why. You can disagree with one if you wish; just explain why you disagree.

Chapter 13 Better Communicators are Organized

A. Define all the vocabulary words on the last page of the chapter.
B. Explain why indentation and specific symbols are used in outlines and why only one idea is given per line.
C. List the steps in creating an outline from the inside out.
D. Give the characteristics of a specific speech purpose.
E. Explain the difference between main points and sub-points.
F. Give the three benefits of parallel sentence structure.
G. List and briefly describe the five informative organizational patterns discussed in the text.
H. Draw the image that shows the placement of the Magic Line, and write on either side of the line the specific qualities of the ideas that fall in the "I zone" and the "E zone".
I. List and briefly describe the eight types of evidence.
J. Explain the difference between figurative and literal analogies.
K. Explain ways to indicate a direct quote when giving a speech aloud.
L. Explain the difference between factual and hypothetical illustrations.
M. List some types of speaking aids and explain why you need low-tech options when giving a speech.
N. Explain how culture can cause a student to accidentally plagiarize.
O. Give the three ways to transition from one Roman numeral to another and tell which one is best.
P. List and briefly explain the purposes of the introduction.
Q. List and briefly explain the purposes of the conclusion.
R. List and briefly explain the four types of credibility.
S. Explain why the title should be short, original, and suggest the topic without revealing it.
T. Give the ethical implication given in the chapter that seemed most important to you and explain why. You can disagree with one if you wish; just explain why you disagree.

Chapter 14 Better Communicators are Confident

A. Define all the vocabulary words on the last page of the chapter.
B. Explain what adrenaline does.

C. Explain the difference between situational anxiety and trait anxiety.
D. Give a couple of physical ways that anxiety affects you.
E. Explain how breathing incorrectly can cause problems when speaking and how correct breathing can help.
F. List four suggestions for physically dealing with speech anxiety.
G. List and briefly explain two mental sources of trait anxiety and how they can produce a self-fulfilling prophecy.
H. Explain how positive imagery helps speaking anxiety.
I. Explain the difference between the verbal code, vocal code, and visual code.
J. Give some tips for increasing immediacy behaviors that help our connection with the audience.
K. Explain how purposeful movement and gestures help speech presentation.
L. Explain how eye contact and voice use help speech presentation.
M. List four elements of vocal delivery.
N. Give some tips on how to effectively use visual aids.
O. Give the ethical implication given in the chapter that seemed most important to you and explain why. You can disagree with one if you wish; just explain why you disagree.

Chapter 15 Better Communicators are Persuasive

A. Define all the vocabulary words on the last page of the chapter.
B. Explain the difference between sympathy and empathy.
C. Give three tasks that are important for persuasive speakers.
D. Give an example from your past of a situation in which you used persuasion in real life.
E. List and briefly explain the three reasons for giving a persuasive speech.
F. Draw the graphic in the text that shows each of the latitudes from Social Judgement Theory.
G. List and briefly explain Aristotle's proofs (appeals).
H. List and briefly explain the four types of credibility.
I. Briefly explain why Aristotle considered proofs a three-legged stool.
J. List and briefly explain the fallacies listed in the text.
K. Create a syllogism with all three elements.
L. List and briefly explain the purpose of the three types of propositions.
M. List each of the persuasive organizational patterns and apply it with Roman numerals only.
N. Give the ethical implication given in the chapter that seemed most important to you and explain why. You can disagree with one if you wish; just explain why you disagree. (252)

Appendix A Speaking at Special Occasions

A. Define all the vocabulary words on the last page of the appendix.

Appendix B Ace the Interview

A. Define all vocabulary terms.

B. When might you engage in a selection interview besides for employment?
C. What two questions would you ask yourself in a self-analysis?
D. When do prospective employers form their first impression of you?
E. Explain the CAR acronym.
F. What should you do *after* the interview to make yourself stand out from other applicants?

Appendix C Maslow's Hierarchy in Relationships and Persuasion

A. Draw the graphic of Maslow's Hierarchy of Needs.
B. Briefly explain Maslow's theory as it affects our actions in meeting our needs.
C. Briefly explain how this theory can affect our understanding of others.
D. Briefly explain how this theory could be used to aid persuasion.

Appendix D Good/Better Communicators are Media Savvy

A. Define all the vocabulary words on the last page of the appendix.
B. Give the purpose of mass media in the United States.
C. List and briefly explain three basic functions of media.
D. Explain how selective exposure and selective retention can interact to prevent people from understanding people with different viewpoints.
E. List and briefly describe two effects of mass media.
F. Give the ethical implication given in the chapter that seemed most important to you and explain why. You can disagree with one if you wish; just explain why you disagree.

Unit One
Assignments and Activities

Self-Introduction Speech

The purposes and the instructions of the self-introduction speech vary. See one set of purposes and instructions below followed by a few of the possible variations.

Purpose: To gain confidence speaking publicly

Instructions: Tell about your past, present and future. Avoid obvious facts. For example, telling us that you are a student at this university dilutes the vividness and power of your presentation.

1. Use 60 seconds.
2. Begin and end with confidence.
   a. steady, still stance
   b. eye contact
   c. clear articulation of your first and last name
3. Use at least one visual aid.
   a. The visual may or may not be electronic.
      i. An electronic visual might be a power point.
      ii. A non-electronic visual might be your basketball.
   b. The visual should be seen be all the audience at one time, not passed around.
   c. The speaker should not say the words, "visual aid".
4. Use no notes.

Variations:

- Take a personality test and include the results in your speech.
- Announce before your speech your personal goal for the speech such as to avoid vocal fillers, to maintain eye contact, avoid crossing ankles.
- Introduce a classmate instead of yourself.

Requirements:
- No paperwork is required.
- No special dress is required.
- Record your speech on your personal devise.

Annotated Bibliography

Purpose: to prepare for the informative speech, the persuasive speech or both

Possible speech topic (something you already know or want to learn about)	10%
3 varied, primary, credible, print sources for the topic, in APA format • "Primary" excludes general encyclopedias and Wikipedia • "Credible" generally excludes blogs and tabloids. 'Credible' usually includes .gov and .edu sources. • Online sources are considered "print" if they are also available in print.	60% (20 pts each)
1 to 4 sentences about the appropriateness of each source for your topic or examples from the source that will bolster your main points.	30% (10 pts each)
See Owl.Purdue for more samples and instruction. https://owl.purdue.edu/owl/research_and_citation/apa_style/apa_formatting_and_style_guide/reference_list_basic_rules.html	

Tear out and staple this page on top of your hard copy, also submit to dropbox.

Example:

Topic: Virtual Reality for Private, Christian University Communication Courses

Payton, K., Scott, J.A. (2013). Communication apprehension among homeschooled college freshmen.

FOCUS on Colleges, Universities & Schools, 7(1), 1-10

> Payton and Scott's work relate to private, Christian university communication courses because private, Christian universities have a relatively high percent of freshman from homeschooled backgrounds. This work shows that the homeschooled population has no more communication apprehension than any other population.

Ridong, H., Yi-Yong, W., Chich-Jen, S. (2016). Effects of virtual reality integrated creative thinking instruction on students' creative thinking abilities. *Eurasia Journal of Mathematics, Science & Technology Education,* 12 (3), 477-486.

> Ridong et.al purport that students who are exposed to or who use virtual reality are more fluent in creative thinking.

Thornhill-Miller, B., DuPont, J. (2016). Virtual reality and the enhancement of creativity and innovation: under recognized potential among converging technologies? *Journal of Cognitive Education & Psychology,* 15(1), 102-121.

> Thornhill-Miller and DuPont suggest that using virtual reality often modifies perceptions of the self and optimizes learning. When the speaker is more confident (self-perception) and relaxed (optimized learning) then the audience is more receptive to the message. Practicing with VR allows the student to gain confidence and relaxation.

Student name:_____Section #:_____Due date: _____

More than an average of 3 errors per page or 3 errors on page one = 0%.

Judgmental versus Reflective Listening

Adapted from Instructor's Manual to accompany Communicating Effectively sixth edition by Saundra Hybels and Richard L. Weaver II, prepared by Renva Watterson, published by McGraw Hill 2001

Purpose: To discern advantages and disadvantages of reflective listening

Procedure:

1. Divide half the class into "persons with problems" and the other half into "problem solvers." Ask each person with a problem to pair up with a problem solver. Assign 1/3 of the persons with problems the role of 1A and his/her problem solver 1B (see below). Assign another 1/3 of the persons with problems the role of 2A and his/her problem solver 2B. Assign the last 1/3 of persons with problems the role of 3A and his/her problem solver 3B.

2. Ask each dyad to do what their situations indicate, saying what the scenario suggests for approximately 2 minutes. Ask two or three dyads to speak their exchanges aloud as the rest of the class listens in. After each dyad has finished with the problem, discuss how the problem was solved and whether the person with the problem felt s/he was helped by the problem-solver. Ask how the persons with problems felt when told s/he "should not feel that way." Make a "Things Not To Do" list.

3. Choose a dyad to simulate the roles in 4A and 4B. Make a "Things To Do" list for reflective listening.

4. Discuss: What are the advantages and disadvantages of reflective listening?

1A You are depressed and find it hard to get out of bed in the morning. You don't know what us causing this depression, but you know that you are getting very little pleasure out of life. You fantasize about leaving town and going to a place where nobody knows you and starting all over again. However, you don't have the energy to do this.

1B Strongly stress that this person *should not* feel the way he/she does. Do not focus on the depression. Instead, give this person a variety of reasons for not feeling depressed, for example, the season is beautiful, classes are stimulating, there are all sorts of interesting things to do on campus. Let this person know it's counterproductive to feel sorry for him/herself.

2A You are working part time on a job where you are making a good salary but your boss is driving you crazy. It seems you can't do anything right; he finds something to criticize almost every day. You are making a lot of effort to do the job to the best of your ability, but you are beginning to feel that you should quit. However, you don't think you can find another job where you can make as much money.

2B   *Give specific advice.* Tell this person to quit the job—that no one has to get along with an unpleasant boss. Also suggest that this person should be clear and specific about all the things that are wrong at work. Say that you are certain that there are other good jobs available. One just has to go out and look for them.

3A   You have been dating the same person for the last 3-4 years. Although both of you have gone to different colleges (400 miles apart), you have agreed that you will not date anyone else. Also, the two of you have been discussing marriage but have decided you should finish school first. Now that you have been at school a few months you are beginning to doubt if you want to stick to the no-dating arrangement. You don't want to break off your relationship, but you are finding it's a drag to sit around weekends while everyone else is having a good time.

3B   Convince the other person that s/he *is wrong* about wanting to date other people. Give a lecture on loyalty and faithfulness. Then tell the person how someone broke off a relationship with you and how it has ruined your life. Try to keep control of the conversation by *talking about yourself* and your experiences.

4A   You are homesick. You miss the comfort of your home, the understanding of your friends, and the support you get from your parents. You never wanted to go away to college, but you came to this school because it has a major you want. Now you are doubting whether the program is worth all the misery you are feeling. You have almost decided to transfer to a school in your hometown. It doesn't have you major so you would have to switch to another program.

4B   On the basis of what you have learned from the other problems discussed in these role plays, try not to make the same mistakes. Make an attempt to *help this person find out what he or she wants to do.* Specifically try not to make any judgements, do not discount the other person's feelings, avoid advice, and do not monopolize the conversation. Support the other person, your goal is to *help him/her examine the options that are open and arrive at a solution s/he will find acceptable (even though it might not be acceptable to you).*

Exam I Review: Ch. 1-5

<u>Type</u> 5 multiple-choice exam questions based on the workbook objectives assigned below.

- At the end of each "stem", include the Ch. #, Obj. letter, and page # from the textbook of the answer.
- Type 5 options: a, b, c, d, e for each question.
- All options must be plausible.
- Write or type the answers tiny and upside down at the end of the fifth question.
- Bring the five questions to class on_____for your classmates' review.
- Head your paper with your name, professor's name, section number, and date due.

Question stem	1		
Chapter #	1		
Objective letter	1		
Page # of the answer	1		
5 plausible answers	5		
Answers (at the end of all 5)	1	=	10 points per question x 5 questions = 50 grading points

Ex. from Ch. 6

1. Which of the following is **NOT** one of the benefits of sharing sensitive, personal information? (6C: 79)
   a. Your secret may spread to others without your consent.
   b. The act of telling your secret may inspire the other person to trust you.
   c. You may feel relief after telling your secret.
   d. You may gain a new perspective after telling your secret.
   e. You may be healthier after telling your secret.

(After you've printed all five of your multi-choice questions, then turn the last page upside down and use small print to write the question #s with the answer to each question.)

Use the chart below to assign a set of five objectives to each student. Student #1 = Ch. 1 obj. BCDEF. Student #2 = Ch. 1 obj. GHIJK. Student #11 writes his/her own set of questions for the same set of objectives as Student #1. In class, students exchange papers to review.

Student # (print names)	Set of objectives		Student # (print names)	Set of objectives
1	Ch. 1 BCDEF		6	Ch. 3 FGHIJ
11			16	
2	Ch. 1 GHIJK		7	Ch. 4 BCDEF
12			17	
3	Ch. 1 L, Ch. 2 BCDE		8	Ch. 4 GHIJ, Ch. 5 B
13			18	
4	Ch. 2 FGHIJ		9	Ch. 5 CDEFG
14			19	
5	Ch. 2 K, Ch. 3 BCDE		10	Ch. 5 HIJK and one
15			20	vocabulary word

Unit Two
Interpersonal Communication

Group Presentation Overview

Planned and rehearsed outside of class

Day & Date:	Day & Date:	Day & Date:	Day & Date:
P. 149 - middle of 157	P. middle of 157-164	P. 169 – middle of 178	P. middle of 178-184
Group 1 members' names	Group 2 members' names	Group 3 members' names	Group 4 members' names

Objectives:
- Use the textbook and **workbook objectives** to present portions of assigned chapters above.
- Apply communication concepts while preparing this **18-20 minute** group presentation.

Preparation:
- Agree on a goal for this group presentation.
- Agree on a few meeting times and places (MWF am or pm, TTH am or pm, Weekend am or pm)
- Choose officers and assign tasks (Tasks may later be traded among members) such as:
  - ✓ Communication: Set time, location, individual goals for each meeting and tasks for each member. Record and distribute information to members.
  - ✓ Compliance to Presentation rubric items 1-5. Ascertain that each rubric point is addressed.
  - ✓ Compliance to Presentation rubric items 6-9 and timing.
  - ✓ Compliance with Group Reflection: Ascertain that each point is complete.
  - ✓ Compliance to "Interpersonal Skills" rubric

Grading: Each student receives two grades, 100 points each:
- A presentation grade determined by the faculty for overall quality of the whole presentation.
  - ✓ Presentation rubric: p._____.
  - ✓ Group members receive the same presentation grade.
- An individual grade determined by the average of each of the group's member's assessment of his/her contribution according to the "Socially Adept 4B" rubric p._____,_____.
  - ✓ Every member will grade him/herself and all other team members.
  - ✓ Every member will receive a unique, individual grade.
  - ✓ **Every late submission receives a 10 point deduction per business day to the individual.**

Paperwork:
- A completed, confidential "Socially Adept 4B" sheet (front and back p._____) **OR** url from each individual group member assessing each member including him/herself
- A copy of the Group Reflection p._____ completed after the presentation from each individual with **the individual's heading** at the top and **personal paragraph** at the end

Group Presentation Reflection

This is one of the 4 reflections that comprise the 200 point, "Reflections" grade.

Purpose: to define values and solve potential problems in future groups.

Procedure: The first part of the Reflection is generated during a group meeting after the presentation. The last part of the Reflection is completed after the group meeting when the individual includes a heading and personal paragraph.

Due:_____(one week after the presentation)

Group Presentation Reflection

As a group, at the post-presentation meeting, prepare a document that includes these elements in this order, and then **email it to each individual group member**.

Title: "Corporate and Individual Reflection of the Group Presentation of (type a name that describes the set of topics you were assigned to teach in your project.)"

1. The alphabetical list of group members with the office and task assigned to each member
2. The chapter #, which ½ of the chapter (first or last), your group # (1, 2, 3, or 4)
3. Each assigned workbook objective, both the labels and the words
4. Five multiple-choice exam questions (five options for each) from the objectives.
5. **The goal(s) determined by the group**
6. An outline of the final plan for your presentation (Your plan to engage the audience with each objective: who will do what)
7. **A schedule of planning meetings (When, Where, How long, Who attended, came late, left early)**
8. A group self-evaluation done at a post-presentation meeting answering four questions.
   a. How close did you come to meeting your goals?
   b. What were your greatest accomplishments?
   c. What changes would you make?
   d. What grade would you give to this presentation?

As an individual, after the group has emailed the above document to you, open that email, copy and paste it onto a new, blank document.

1. At the top, type the heading:
   Your name
   Professor's name
   Course and section number
   Date that this reflection is due
2. At the end of the group's document, type two paragraphs about what you personally learned, then submit a single document with your heading, the group report and your paragraphs to your professor.
   a. Type the first paragraph about what you learned in relation to the task you were assigned (from the Group Presentation Overview document: either the communication task or one of the compliance tasks).
   b. Type the second paragraph about any other learning from the content of the chapter, about the dynamics of group work, etc.
3. Complete both sides of the **confidential** "Socially Adept Interpersonal Skills 4b" or the url. Submit it to your professor.

More than an average of 3 errors per page or 3 errors on page one = 0%.

Group Presentation   Date_____ Group #_____Section #_____

Names: _____   _____

_____   _____

1. Dress: appropriate costume or professional (no jeans, no open-back shoes)	1 2 3 4 5
2. Elocution: clear enunciation, appropriate pronunciation, volume, and rate	1 2 3 4 5
3. Beginning: introduced presenters, the general topic, and **the sequence of events**, generated interest	1 2 3 4 5
4. Visuals: managed skillfully, attractive and legible, each vocabulary item was displayed while it was being taught	1 2 3 4 5
5. Respect: attentive to members of the group and the audience, used only professional or appropriate language	1 2 3 4 5
6. Content: **demonstrated** or engaged the audience with **all objectives** and **vocabulary** in a memorable way, such as skits and audience participation; used **neither lecture nor discussion nor verbal examples** (counts 2x)	1,2,3,4,5,6 7,8 9,10
7. Assessment: quizzed each student over **each objective and vocab. word** during the 20 min. presentation with easy-to-understand questions and answers	1 2 3 4 5
8. Equity: equal appearance of responsibilities among the members	1 2 3 4 5
9. Ending: easy-to-remember, concise summary of the main point (1 phrase or sentence)	1 2 3 4 5

Subtotal _____

Less any timing violation (18-20 min.) _____**GROUP GRADE** _____

For every 15 second interval under 18 minutes or beyond 20 minutes, one point will be deducted. For example, a 17-minute presentation loses 4 points; a 20-minute-and-1-second presentation loses 1 point.

This group grade will be assigned to each member. Additionally, each member will receive a unique individual grade after s/he submits the Group Reflection and a completed "4B Socially Adept Interpersonal Skills in Group Settings" rubric.

Dress to Impress

You never get a second chance to make a first impression. In many cases, the audience decides how much attention they will pay to you based on your appearance. We can't please all the people all the time, but we can follow a general wardrobe guideline to make the best impression on most of the people most of the time. That guideline is to dress either in costume or one level above the average dress of the audience.

DRESS EITHER IN COSTUME OR ONE LEVEL ABOVE THE AVERAGE DRESS OF THE AUDIENCE.

"In costume" means that if you are presenting the advantages of a study abroad program in Paris, you might wear a French themed outfit, perhaps with a beret. Are you presenting on a controversy in professional tennis? Look for a blazer and slacks that resemble those worn by the officials at Wimbledon. Demonstrate how to paint a tree in paint-stained casual clothes that are typically worn in an artist's studio.

"One level above the average dress of the audience" on a college campus may or may not be "profession-al". Professional is a step above the collared shirt and nice jeans for men and above the fitted t-shirt and fitted jeans for women. Professional dress is more polished that slide-on shoes. Professional shoes have a full back or a back strap. Professional dress includes a top, a bottom and a third piece. That third piece may be a sweater, jacket, vest, scarf, or tie. Jewelry is conservative.

♀ For women, tops have sleeves and higher necklines. Both trousers and skirts are appropriate. The skirt length extends to the knee or beyond unless opaque tights are worn to cover the legs. Leggings are professional if they are covered down to the thigh by the blouse, shirt, or sweater. Some open-toe shoes are professional enough, athletic shoes are not.

♂ For men, khakis or dress slacks are more professional than corduroys. Relaxed shoes and loafers are appropriate; athletic shoes are not. Shirts and ties may be either conservative colors or bright and patterned.

© BeeBeeKiller/Shutterstock.com

Figure 1 Which one of these women is NOT wearing professional dress?

Interpersonal Skills in Group Settings

Complete both sides. On the reverse, circle a # for each criterion, for each member, **including yourself.** Information on this side is **NOT** used for grading.

Rank each member of your group including yourself based on their value/contribution.

1. Most contribution_____

2. _____

3. _____

4. _____

5. Least contribution _____

What else should the professor know about this group? _____
_____
_____
_____

Mark as many descriptions as are appropriate in each of these three columns. **In our group, I...**

Task Roles:

__Set meeting time/place
__Checked the rubric
__Shared facts & opinions
__Typed Post Pres. Reflection
__Recorded group decisions
__Kept the group on task
__Coordinated group & individual activities
__Sought information and opinions from the group members

Maintenance Roles:

__Helped solve conflict
__Provided food
__Relieved tension
__Supported others
__Helped everyone to participate

Disruptive Roles:

__Sought recognition
__Dominated the discussion
__Blocked group efforts
__Did not participate

Mark the descriptions that apply to your group in these four columns.

In our group, the leader:

__emerged
__was appointed by the faculty
__was elected by the group
__did not exist-we were leaderless

The conclusions reached by our group were:

__ made by consensus
__ made by majority vote
__ made by the minority
__ made by the leadership

Our group goals were:

__antagonistic
__complimentary
__agreed upon by all
__clear

The group conflict included:

__procedure
__power
__work distribution
__substance, important issues

List the tasks that you personally accomplished.

_____
_____
_____

Two people can accomplish more than twice as much as one...If one falls, the other can help. Ecclesiastes 4:9-10

The grade I honestly believe I earned is_____ % Signature_____

Printed name_____Group # 1, 2, 3, 4, 5 Section #_____Date____/____/_____

4B Whole Person Assessment   Socially Adept

Interpersonal Skills in Group Settings last names, including yours, alphabetical:

		4 Exemplary	3 Competent	2 Acceptable	1 Unacceptable	0 Not Attempted					
N O N - V E R B A L		Always • Improved community with attire, tone, touch, expressions, proximity, food, or gifts, etc. • Pursued excellence contagiously	Always • Improved the community with attire, tone, touch, expressions, and proximity	50% of the time • Used appropriate attire, tone, touch, expressions, and proximity	Often • Distracted with clothing, voice, odor, touching, sitting or talking too close or far away	Never interacted with the group	4 3 2 1 0	4 3 2 1 0	4 3 2 1 0	4 3 2 1 0	4 3 2 1 0
C I V I L I T Y		Always • Spoke honestly and kindly, no profanity • Personalized communication without too much time off-task • Distributed work evenly • Helped others	Almost always • Spoke honestly and kindly no profanity • Personalized communication without too much time off - task • Distributed work evenly	50% of the time • Spoke honestly and kindly • Spoke with others as individuals	Often • Used profanity, stereotypes, etc. • Blocked progress with too much/little personal info or humor • Favored unfair workloads	Never interacted with the group	4 3 2 1 0	4 3 2 1 0	4 3 2 1 0	4 3 2 1 0	4 3 2 1 0
R E S P E C T		Consistently • Participated with and trusted others across gender, culture and/or other differences	Almost always • Valued other genders, cultures etc. • Listened to members who were different	50% of the time • May have been uncomfortable yet avoided conflict	Often • Treated differences as deficiencies • Excluded contributions from others	Never interacted with the group	4 3 2 1 0	4 3 2 1 0	4 3 2 1 0	4 3 2 1 0	4 3 2 1 0
C O N T R I B U T I O N		Consistently • Presented fresh, relevant info, services, or materials • Accomplished more than assigned &/or greater quality • Arrived early • Averted unhelpful distractions	Almost always • Presented fresh, relevant info, services, or materials • Accomplished more than assigned &/or greater quality • Arrived early • Averted distractions	50% of the time • Presented relevant information, services, or materials • Finished assignments timely & well • Avoided distractions	Often • Promoted irrelevant, redundant, or impractical points, materials, services, or nothing • Argued over trivia	Presented no information, service, or material	4 3 2 1 0	4 3 2 1 0	4 3 2 1 0	4 3 2 1 0	4 3 2 1 0
C O N F L I C T **M A N A G E M E N T**		Consistently, quickly • Identified and • Managed all conflicts directly and bias-free with – accommodation – compromise – collaboration or – persuasion	Almost always • Identified and • Managed conflicts bias- free with – accommodation – compromise, – collaboration, or – persuasion	50% of the time • Acknowledged and • Managed conflicts without prejudice	Often • Used – contempt – coercion – passive-aggression – silence &/or – defensiveness – insisted that a problem was insurmountable or non-existent.	Never interacts with the group	4 3 2 1 0	4 3 2 1 0	4 3 2 1 0	4 3 2 1 0	4 3 2 1 0

The Information Gathering Interview

Be prepared to share your answers. Complete all 4 pages for 25 grading items.
Four pages of instructions and examples follow these 4 worksheet pages.

Student name_____ Section #_____ Date_____

1. Possible topic for your informative &/or your persuasive speech:

_____

2. Name of the person or position that you think you can interview. Describe the person's expertise.

_____

Read about your topic, narrow your focus, and then **write 3 questions** (worth 3 points each, 9 points total) that all apply to the same interview. Each of the 3 questions should have all four of the following qualities:

A. Informed
- o If the answer is easily available online, then the question is NOT "informed".
- o You may write a statement followed by a question.
  - ▪ Tell the interviewee what you have read, seen or heard,
  - ▪ then ask for his/her opinion or experience.

B. Open-ended
- o If the answer can be a single word or short phrase such as "yes" or "no" or "The fourth of July" then the question is NOT open.
- o Begin questions with "How" "Why" and sometimes "What" to invite interesting explanations and stories.

C. Precise
- o If you ask two questions in one then the question is NOT "precise".
- o Ask a single question at a time.

D. Unbiased/Objective
- o If the phrasing of the question supports or prompts a particular view point, then the question is NOT "Unbiased/Objective".
- o Get more reliable and sometimes surprising insights from interviewees by making it easy for the interviewee to express any opinion.

E. Uses commonly understood vocabulary

1st question worth 3 pts. 3,4,5.	
2nd question worth 3 pts. 6,7,8.	
3rd question worth 3 pts. 9,10,11.	

The Selection Interview

Go to monster.com. Read any of the articles about being interviewed for a job. Record the author, title, some facts from the article and what you were thinking as you read it.

12. Article's Author:

_____

13. Article's Title:

_____

14. Facts from the article:

_____

_____

_____

15. Your thoughts and/or feelings about the Monster article:

_____

_____

_____

_____

_____

In the next section of this exercise, you will no longer be preparing an information-gathering interview. Instead you will practice using the CAR method of responding to questions that may be asked of you in a selection (employment or scholarship) interview, when someone is asking questions of you.

The CAR method is designed for "behavioral questions" that begin with "Tell me about a time when you…" You can also use the CAR method to be specific and memorable even if the question does not begin with, "Tell me about a time when you…"

You can be more memorable, and you can describe your strengths without bragging when you tell short, purposeful stories from your real life.

Student Name_____Section #_____Date _____

Page 3 of the 4-page Interview homework

"Tell me about a time when you were especially motivated to do good work." or "What motivates you?"

Write each part of your answer in the cells below. Find examples on the following pages in this workbook.

16.	Short answer	Examples: I am motivated by verbal recognition, winning an award, $, family, the team, children, fear of failure, or of causing others trouble, etc. Write your short answer here, in this box.
17.	**C**ontext your authentic, concrete, specific problem, told in past tense **C**	For a "concrete, specific" problem, instead of writing, "For instance, I was once in a fast-paced work environment" say, "For instance last semester, when I was working at Wendy's during the lunch-time mega-rush…"
18.	**A**ction specific, concrete actions you per-formed in the situation described in "C" **A**	
19.	**R**esult tangible results that occurred from your actions **R**	
20.	Repeat the short answer	

42

Student Name_____Section #_____Date _____
Page 4 of the 4-page interview homework.

"Tell me about a time when you had to deal with conflict between yourself and someone at work." Or "How do you handle conflict between yourself and another person?"

Write each part of your answer in the cells below. Find examples on the following pages in this workbook.

21.	Short answer	If you have no work-conflict stories, tell a volunteer-conflict or some other conflict story. Write your short answer in this box.
22.	**C**ontext your authentic, con-crete, specific conflict, told in past tense **C**	"For instance…"
23.	**A**ction specific, concrete ac-tions you performed in the situation described in "C" **A**	
24.	**R**esult tangible results that occurred from your actions **R**	
25.	Repeat the short answer	

Examples of the Interview Homework
from the previous pages

The following boxes are adapted from Dobkin and Pace (2006) *Communication in a Changing World* published by McGraw Hill.

The homework and these examples are about two different kinds of interviews, the information- gathering interview and the selection interview. Use information-gathering interviews to prepare speeches. An interview is required for both the informative speech and the persuasive speech. Use the selection interview to be chosen for a scholarship, internship, employment, etc.

The first 5 boxes of examples contrast poorly worded information-gathering questions with better questions. They apply to page one of your homework.

The final 3 boxes are examples of appropriate and efficient ways to answer questions in a selection interview. They apply to the final 2 pages of your homework and to your next scholarship/internship/employment opportunity!

1 **Uninformed** (worse)	**Informed** (better)
How do you like being an attorney?	Why do you practice civil law instead of criminal law?
Is getting into law school hard?	When applying to law school, is it more important to have a good grade point average or a high score on the LSAT?
Do you make a lot of money?	What are the advantages of requiring a retainer before you take a case compared to working off a commission?

2 **Closed** (worse)	**Open** (better)
Did you think you were going to win the race?	What were you thinking just before the race started?
Are you patriotic?	How do you show patriotism in your life?
Are the Beatles the greatest rock band of all time?	Why are the Beatles your favorite band?

Interview homework examples continue on the next page.

3	**Double-Barreled Question** (worse)	**One Question at a Time** (better)
	Do you think the country is heading into a recession and should the federal government lower the interest rate to help the downturn in the economy?	How does lowering the interest rate help prevent a recession?
	Do you think the university should offer a major in ethnic studies, because doesn't such a major help people understand each other better?	How would a major in ethnic studies benefit the university?

4	**Leading** (worse)	**Objective** (better)
	Most students dislike the university's pass/fail policy. What do you think?	What do you think of the university's pass/fail policy?
	The new fall fashions seem so bulky and uncomfortable. Do you like them?	What is your opinion of the new fall fashions?
	We have such a parking problem on campus. Don't you think we should build a new parking garage?	What are the advantages of building a new parking garage on campus?

5	**Hard to Understand Vocabulary** (worse)	**More Accessible Language** (better)
	How often do you watch **CMT**?	How often do you watch the **Country Music Channel**?
	Do you agree with the **new law** on child safety seats?	How do you feel about the **new law that requires children under the age of four to be restrained in a safety seat**?

Interview homework examples continue.

Use the following examples to prepare for a selection interview.

If you are asked, "What are some of your strengths?" You might reply with one or more of the following three CAR-styled answers to be memorable without bragging.

What are some of your strengths?

Short answer	I am very organized.
Context	For instance, this semester I carried 18 units, wrote for the campus newspaper, and worked 20 hours a week at a part-time job.
Action	Using a daily planner, I scheduled my time carefully, including reserving blocks of hours for study and tracking my assignments on a project manager.
Results	Even though this was my hardest semester, I earned my highest grade point average ever and was selected to the dean's honor roll.
Repeat the short answer	I am very organized.

What are some of your strengths?

Short answer	I take initiative in solving problems.
Context	For instance, last year I noticed that our campus did not have a recycling program for classroom buildings and offices. Students were throwing aluminum cans and glass bottles into the regular trash.
Action	I approached the student senate with a plan that called for a recycling canister to be placed in every classroom building. I estimated the cost of the program and arranged for a local company to collect the items to be recycled and share the profits. The senate approved the plan and budgeted enough money for a trial program in the largest buildings.
Results	We made enough money on the trial program to expand the effort to every building on campus.
Repeat the short answer	I take initiative in solving problems.

Interview homework examples continue.

What are some of your strengths?

Short answer	I am good at delegating responsibility.
Context	I work at a large department store and I was in charge of our United Way giving campaign last year. We have over 300 employees. I couldn't talk with each one individually and an announcement in the employee newsletter seemed too impersonal.
Action	I sought out reliable volunteers from each department within the store to be group leaders. I held two training sessions where I reviewed the value of the program and taught the group leaders how to approach colleagues for donations. I made two follow-up phone calls during the campaign to each group leader to offer encouragement and to check the status of the campaign.
Results	With very little investment of my own time, we had the most successful campaign in recent years.
Repeat the short answer	I am good at delegating responsibility.

Communication and Leadership Reflection

This is one of the 4 reflections that comprise the 200 point "Reflections Grade".

Purpose: To synthesize professional and personal goals, anticipate and plan to neutralize obstacles

Procedure: Type a four paragraph essay. Some professors want this page stapled above the essay.

1. The first of the four paragraphs is about the student's **personal and/or family goals.**
   - It includes **3 specific and achievable communication and leadership skills** necessary for success in his/her personal and/or family life.
   - According to Sapir and Whorf, we can think about things better when we have a name for them. Therefore a name for each of the three skills is highlighted in color. (Gray is a color.) Any skills named in the textbook or workbook are acceptable. For example: Listening for information is a skill from the textbook's chapter on listening and Perception checking is a skill from the chapter about being considerate. /10

2. The second of the four paragraphs requires the student to name his/her likely, **future career.**
   - It includes **3 specific and achievable communication and leadership skills** necessary for success in that career. The skills may be the same as or different from those listed in the personal/family goals. Any skills named in the textbook or workbook are acceptable.
   - A name of each of those three skills is highlighted in color. /10

3. The third of the four paragraphs is about the **obstacle(s)** that stand(s) in the way of achieving these communication and leadership goals.
   - The name(s) of the obstacle(s) is highlighted in color. For example: An obstacle to listening for information is my neglect of looking for an over-arching structure in the other person's conversation. An obstacle for perception checking is my self-serving bias. /10

4. The fourth of the four paragraphs is about the student's **action plan** to overcome each obstacle. Highlight the WHEN words in color.
   - The actions...
     - are observable
     - are realistic
     - have measurable results
     - include a timeline. For example, say that you will practice paying attention to over-arching structure in your roommate's conversations **on the way back to the dorm from church each week.** /10

5. Details
   - **Title**: "Communication and Leadership Reflection".
   - **Length**: at least one whole and no more than two pages
   - **Error free**: typographical, spelling, grammatical, punctuation.
   - **Concluding single sentence** is the most important lesson the student is learning about communication and leadership. /10

Total_____/50 points _____%

Student name:_____Section #_____Date due:_____

See example on next page.

More than an average of 3 errors per page or more than 3 errors on page one = 0%.

48

Student's Name_____
Instructor's Name_____
COM 101 Section #_____
Date____

Communication and Leadership Reflection

According to John Maxwell, the definition of leadership is influence. However, to influence others, one must be able to communicate well. Successful communication starts in my personal life. Whether in my friendships or family, one skill that I want to work on is active listening. When I listen to others, I show them that I value what they have to say, which is crucial for building relationships and leading intentionally. Another skill I would like to work on is attribution, the act of trying to interpret what someone else meant by their words or actions. To avoid miscommunication, I want to ensure that I understand others' intentions. The last skill that I want to work on is chronemics, the messages that my time management sends. Because efficient time management is critical in American culture, I not only want to be respectful of others' time but also set an example of successful management.

All those skills are transferrable to my future career as an English teacher because my interactions with students are just as meaningful. When I am engaging in conversation with my students, I want to utilize active listening skills. If I expect my students to actively listen to me as I am teaching, I need to be the first to listen to them. This example demonstrates that I care about them. When I care about my students on a relational level, I will improve my ability to attribute correctly. Being aware of various factors that contribute to student achievement and behavior will help me to adjust my teaching to meet their needs. Lastly, something I want to be aware of as a teacher is perceptual constancy, which is the difficulty in perceiving someone differently even after he or she changes. As my students learn and grow throughout the year, I want to view them based on how they have grown rather than how they used to be.

When acquiring any new skill, there are always obstacles to overcome. During a lecture or conversation, I tend to overthink the content, leading to distraction. This distraction is a type of internal interference. The other kind of interference is external, which affects my chronemics. I often get distracted by certain tasks, which causes me to be late frequently. Another obstacle that I face in reaching the goals listed above is the fundamental attribution error, which is when I think that someone's negative words or actions are a result of their character rather than external circumstances. This error leads to both wrong attribution and perceptual constancy.

To overcome the obstacle of internal distraction, I can take notes during all my future lectures. If I forget something in conversation with my friends, family, or students, I can ask clarifying questions, rather than missing the rest of their words trying to remember. Before I go to an appointment or meeting, I will allow myself enough time to prepare and get there by making a list of everything I need and researching the travel time. I will also move distractions, like my cell phone, out of my sight while I am getting ready. To avoid the fundamental attribution error, I will ask my friends and students questions about themselves early in our relationships, either in conversation or a survey, to get to know them better. As I earn their trust and learn more about their situations, I can better understand the reasons for their words and actions.

To be an effective communicator and leader, I need to try and perceive situations from others' points of view while also reflecting on how my own words and actions are influencing those around me.

Please see instructions on the previous page.

Mid Term Course Evaluation

Section #_____
Date _____

Instructions:

- Please respond to all the questions below that you feel comfortable responding to at this time.
- You do not need to include your name, but you may include it if you would like.
- When responding, please make sure responses are legible.

1. What do you enjoy about this class?

2. What are you learning in this class?

3. What would you like to see more of in this class?

4. How may I be praying for you?

Unit Three
Public Speaking

Public Speaking: Changing the World

Overview of the public speaking section of the workbook:

The purpose of public speaking	To inform, persuade, or entertain a specific audience about an event, an idea, an object, a process, a person or group by the expression of information, reasoning, and feelings.
The basic 3-part rule of public speaking	1. Tell them what you are going to tell them. 2. Tell them 3. Tell them what you told them.
The meaning of the 3-part rule	Say the main points 3 times, first in the introduction, then in the body and again in the conclusion.
Grading	page_____Outline of the informative speech page_____Oral presentation of the informative speech page_____Outline of the persuasive speech page_____Oral presentation of the persuasive speech
Sample outlines	page_____Sample outline of the informative speech page_____Sample outline of the persuasive speech
Instructions	page_____Instructions for the informative outline page_____Instructions for the persuasive outline page_____Instructions for the oral presentations page_____Instructions for the reflection of the informative speech page_____Instructions for the reflection of the persuasive speech

Audience and Occasion Analysis

Purpose: to connect with particular people at a particular time and place (to free the
speaker from using generic terms and examples).

1. Demographics

Age_____ Race/ethnicity/nationality_____

Gender_____ Group affiliation(s) _____

Education_____ Occupation_____

Religion_____

2. Occasion:

Season of the year_____ Day of the week_____

Sports season_____ Venue_____

Holiday season_____ Venue size_____

Academic season_____ Available technology_____

Time of day _____ Physical comfort level_____

3. Your **informative speech topic**: _____

4. Audience knowledge/anchor belief about this topic(s)?

_____

_____

_____

5. How will the audience relate to this topic(s)? (Why do they care about it?)(Check demographics.)

_____

_____

6. What will your audience be doing or thinking about during the hours just before your speech?

_____

_____

7. What will your audience be doing or thinking about during the hours after your speech?

_____

_____

8. How does the time and place relate to your topic(s)?

_____

_____

9. How will you narrow your topic to fit this audience and occasion?

_____

_____

10. A source of information for your informative speech that this audience will respect or enjoy.

_____

_____

11. Topics in the latitude of rejection for this audience at this time: (See persuasion chapter.)

_____

_____

12. Topics in the latitude of acceptance for this audience at this time: (See persuasion chapter.)

_____

_____

13. Topics in the latitude of non-commitment for this audience at this time: (See persuasion chapter.)

_____

_____

14. A source of information for your persuasive speech that this audience will respect or enjoy.

_____

_____

15. What will the audience expect of the speaker in terms of style? What else will the audience expect?

_____

_____

Ask your Professor for Acceptable Organizational Patterns.

Use Parallel Sentences.

Readers can see italics, paragraph breaks; they can go back and re-read. Audiences can't.
Therefore memorable speakers are simpler and more repetitive than writers. Ex. "I have a dream..."

Parallel sentences are more repetitive, simpler, shorter and often clearer than non-parallel sentences.
The following two examples compare non-parallel points to parallel points over the same content.
Which version seems more organized and easier to remember?

Ex.1.   Noah's Ark Water Park in Wisconsin: (non-parallel) ☹
I.   Noah's Ark Water Park is known for being the largest in the nation.
II.   Some of the most exciting thrill rides combine rollercoasters and slides.
III.   The park also includes a 4D theatre.

(parallel) ☺

I.	Noah's Ark has size.
II.	Noah's Ark has thrills.
III.	Noah's Ark has cinema.

Ex. 2.   Corruption of Political Power: (non-parallel) ☹
I.   Congress can become corrupt.
II.   There have been corrupt members of the executive branch.
III.   Judges may solicit bribes.

(parallel) ☺

I.	Corruption decays Congress.
II	Corruption decays the White House.
III.	Corruption decays the judiciary.

Rhyme and alliteration are optional.

Ex. 1. World Cup Soccer (alliteration)

I.	World Cup Soccer advances kids.
II.	World Cup Soccer advances commitment.
III.	World Cup Soccer advances cash.

Ex. 2. Middle Eastern Beauty (rhyme)

I.	Enjoy the delicious grapes.
II.	Enjoy the fabric drapes.
III.	Enjoy the dramatic escapes.

Write your **main points** (Roman Numerals).

Name a specific college or university library data base that relates to your topic.
_____

Without parallel sentence structure:

Main Point I.

_____

Main Point II.

_____

Main Point III. Optional

_____

Main Point IV .Optional

_____

Main Point V. Optional

_____

With parallel sentence structure: Write a declarative sentence that includes a subject and a predicate. Questions may make good transitions, but questions are not helpful as main points.

Main Point I.

_____

Main Point II.

_____

Main Point III. Optional

_____

Main Point IV Optional

_____

Main Point V. Optional

_____

Write your **sub-points** (Capital Letters) as <u>parallel</u> sentences.

Each main point (Roman numeral) has between two and five sub-points (Capital letters).
The sub-points are parallel with each other and not necessarily parallel with any Roman numeral.

Parallelism works in small groups.
- The <u>main</u> points are parallel with each other. (I. II. III. IV. V.)
- The <u>sub</u>-points under one Roman numeral are parallel with each other. (I. A. B. C. D. E.)
- The <u>sub</u>-points under another Roman numeral are parallel with each other. (II. A. B. C. D. E.)

The main points and sub-points below that share the same font need to be parallel with each other.
See examples of parallelism in the sample informative outline and the sample persuasive outline in this workbook.

Ex.

I. "I" is a full sentence, parallel with II and III only.

    A. "A" is a full sentence, parallel with I. B and I. C only.

        1.

        2.

    B. "B" is a full sentence, parallel with I. A and I. C only.

    C. "C" is a full sentence, parallel with I. A and I. B only.

        1.

        2.

II. "II" is a full sentence, parallel with I and III only

    A. "A" is a full sentence, parallel with II. B and II. C only

    B. "B" is a full sentence, parallel with II. A and II. C only

    C. "C" is a full sentence, parallel with II. A and II. B only

        1.

        2.

        3.

III. "III" is a full sentence, parallel with I and II only

    A. "A" is a full sentence, parallel with III. B only

        1.

        2.

        3.

    B. "B" is a full sentence, parallel with III. A only

        1.

        2.

Support Your Main and Sub-Points.

Use Roman numerals and capital letters for <u>ideas</u>. Use Arabic numerals and lower case letters for proof, evidence, and support.

- Every main-point (Roman numeral) requires 2-5 sub-points.
- Every sub-point (Capital letter) breaks the main-point idea into bite-sized ideas.
- Every sub-sub-point (Arabic numeral) (1, 2, 3) adds proof, support, evidence to the sub point.
  - Main-points and sub-points require complete, parallel sentences.
  - Sub-sub-points do NOT require sentences or parallelism.

Vary the <u>types</u> of support.
- Explanation
  - Definition (may be printed on a visual)
  - Illustration (story)
  - Comparison, contrast, or analogy
  - Examples (first hand, second hand, hypothetical)
- Statistics
  - Prices, dates, numbers may be printed on a visual.
  - Graphs help audiences grasp the concepts.
  - Listing the source and/or date of the statistic bolsters credibility.
- Expert opinion (may be printed on a visual with an image of the expert.)
- Visual aids (In the outline describe the aid and label it, "visual".)
(In the outline it is NOT sufficient to type "1. statistics" or "2. expert opinion." Earn credit by typing in numbers, quotes, paraphrases, etc. in addition to the label.)

The following good example has 5 supports, also called, "evidence" or "proof" for a single main point.

I. The first step to competitive fishing is to research the lake.
   A. Our team researches on-line. *(breaks the main-point into bit-sized pieces)*
      1. Depth of the lake **(example)**
         a. Lake Tenkiller's avg. depth 51' **(stat)**
         b. Grand Lake's avg. depth 33' **(stat)**
      2. Water color and normal visibility **(example)**
         a. Keystone Lake's visibility is average **(visual: glass of keystone water)**
         b. Skiatook Lake's visibility is good **(contrast)**
      3. Normal water temperature for that time of year is about 67° F. **(example)**
   B. Our team researches past tournament results. *(breaks the main-point into bite-sized pieces)*
      1. Zach Vankeulen, previous team captain, recommends contacting professional fishing guides. **(expert)**
      2. Jonathan Williamson, current team captain, recommends contacting the local marina. **(expert)**

Organize three or more pieces of evidence under the sub-points (capital letters) of each main point. Main points are Roman numerals.

Format the Body of the Outline.

> Outlines are not "speaking notes".
> - Outlines convert your audible speech into a visual, graphic picture of a speech.
>   - Outlines show the relationships among the ideas.
>   - Outlines, like parallelism, keep ideas organized and easy to remember.

I. Use Roman numerals for main points.
II. Use other symbols for sub-points and sub-sub-points, etc.
    A. Use capital letters for sub-points, "A.", "B."
        1. Use 2-5 sub-points for each main point.
        2. Use "A." and "B." for sub-points.
    B. Use Arabic numerals for sub-sub-points.
        1. Most main points (Roman Numerals) will use sub-sub points.
        2. The numbers "1", "2", and "3" are Arabic numerals.
    C. Use lower case letters for sub-sub-sub-points.
        1. Use any number of sub-sub-sub-points.
        2. "a" and "b" are lower case and are used for sub-sub-sub points.
        3. A lower case letter further explains information from the Arabic numeral above it.
III. Follow specific rules for symbols, indentions, and groupings.
    A. Use only one symbol per statement.
        1. Use either a letter or a number, not both for one statement.
        2. Do not use "A.1." followed by a statement.
    B. Indent each subordinate level 5 spaces.
        1. A long sentence that takes more than one line begins its second line under the same place that the long sentence began.
        2. Indentions graphically represent your speech.
    C. Use a minimum of two ideas per grouping.
        1. Do not use an "a" without a "b" or a "1" without a "2".
        2. Expand a single idea into two parts.
        3. Eliminate a single idea by incorporating it into its superior heading.
    D. Limit ideas / supports per grouping to five.
IV. Keep numbered/lettered vertical columns straight.
V. Turn off your computer's auto formatting if necessary.

> After you outline the body of your speech, then type the introduction, conclusion, transitions, title and bibliography.

Cut Words that Add Clutter, are Vague, or are not Conversational.
- "you know", "like", "and stuff like that"
- "most people" , "Christians today ", "A study shows"
- "my visual aid", "my interview", "I've researched", or "in my speech today"
- "very"

Introduce your Speech with Three Parts in Paragraph Form.

- Attention
- Credibility and rapport
- Preview

1. Write the attention part of the introduction.

- Statistics (Make statistics more comprehensible by comparing the numbers to something easily recognized such as a football field or the population of your state.)
- Quotation (Make quotations more attention-getting by quoting someone we respect or someone surprising.)
- Anecdote (Not a description, but a story with a beginning, middle and end.)
- Provocative Statement
- Humor

Write an attention step appropriate to yourself, your topic, audience, and occasion.

_____

_____

2. Write the credibility & rapport part of the introduction.

- <u>Credibility</u> is the audience's perception of the speaker's expertise, character, and goodwill.
- <u>Rapport</u> is a harmonious or sympathetic relation.
- Your personal story may be both an anecdote that captures the audience' attention and a credibility and rapport element that makes the audience like and trust you. See samples p.   - .

What can you say, do, wear, show, or give to the audience to establish credibility and rapport?

_____

_____

3. Write the preview part of the introduction.

- Last sentence(s) of the introduction
- Specifies every main point obviously, usually in a single sentence
- Helps the audience to listen for and remember the main points

Ex. Preview: "The role of a manager is to plan, to organize, to direct, and to control."

  I. Managers plan.
  II. Managers organize.
  III. Managers direct.
  IV. Managers control.

Write your main points in a single, preview sentence.

_____

_____

Combine your attention, credibility & rapport, and preview into a paragraph. If necessary, add some background information to finish your introduction.

Conclude your Speech with two Parts in Paragraph Form.

Write the **summary** and **clincher** in a single paragraph.

- The <u>summary</u>, like the preview lists all the specific main points to help the audience remember.
- The <u>clincher</u> is a short, final sentence or phrase that sums up the whole purpose of your speech.

This example reviews four main points and uses the quote, "Something good..." as a clincher:

Example of a speech with 4 main points about Oral Roberts

      I. Oral Roberts became famous for "Seed Faith".

      II. Oral Roberts became famous for healing prayer.

      III. Oral Roberts became famous for Oral Roberts University.

      IV. Oral Roberts became famous for inspirational phrases.

> Conclusion: We have seen that Oral Roberts became famous for "Seed Faith", healing prayer, the University, and telling everyone that, "Something good is going to happen to you!"

This example reviews three main points and uses humor, "it's a hot topic" as a clincher:

Example of a speech with 3 main points about cremation.

      I. Cremation has similar costs to traditional burial.

      II. Cremation has a greater variety of final resting places than traditional burials.

      III. Cremation has opponents.

> Conclusion: When deciding between cremation and traditional burials, remember that cremation costs about the same as a traditional burial, cremation offers a greater variety of final resting places than a traditional burial, but many people have strong feelings against cremation. Cremation, it's a hot topic.

- Avoid all new ideas in the conclusion.
- Avoid "should", "ought", or "must" in an informative conclusion.

Write your conclusion including each individual main point followed by a clincher.

_____

_____

_____

_____

Transition between the Main Points

Summarize the previous part(s) and introduce the next part in a transition.

- **Avoid pronouns** to be clear and to repeat the words that you want the audience to remember.
- **Exclude** support and evidence such as statistics or quotes.
- **Limit** the transition to one, two, or maybe three sentences.
  - After the introduction
  - Between all main points
  - *Before the conclusion.

Two good examples of transitions between the introduction and the first main point on procrastination:

Effective: "Procrastination usually begins like any other habit."

Effective: "First, let's talk about how procrastination begins."

Write a transition to bridge your introduction to your first main point.

_____

The transition between the first and second points of bullying combine both points in a single sentence.

Effective: "Bullying is rampant but there are effective methods to stopping it."

Ineffective: "Now that you know about bullying, let's learn how to contain the problem."

The ineffective example incorrectly assumes that everyone in the audience totally focused and understood everything you said in the previous part.

The first, better example, more realistically reminds the audience of the first point.

Write a transition that summarizes your first main point and introduces your second main point.

_____

_____

*The final transition between the last point and the conclusion summarizes **only** the final main point.

Write a Title to Suggest but not Reveal the Topic.

Topic	Title
Women's soccer	Queen of the Grass
Cave exploration	Journey into Darkness
Peter denies Christ	Oops, I Did it Again
Kevin Durant	The Durantula

Your topic_____ Your title_____

Type your References in APA Style followed by the Interview.

For the interview, type the Last name, First name. Date. "Personal interview". The person's relation to the speech topic

Example of an interview reference in a speech about Chick-Fil-A restaurants:

Johnson, Laura. October 4, 2019. Personal interview. Chick-Fil-A employee

Follow the interview citation with five informed, open, unbiased questions from your interview. The answers to the questions are not required.
See an example of the questions in the Persuasive Speech Sample Outline p._____.

Compare your outline to the "Informative Speech Outline **Sample**" p._____.

Compare your outline to the "Informative Speech Outline **Grading**", p._____.

Tear out the Informative Speech Outline Grading and staple it on top of your outline.

Rehearse with Presentational Aids and Appropriate Dress.

Plan presentational aids.
Rule of thumb: at least one aid for each main point.
- Use audience participation, sight, sound, touch, taste, and/or smell to reinforce and clarify.
- Consider using Power Point, Key Notes, Google Presentations, Prezi, Word Press etc. remembering to
    - Use **minimal text, mostly images** (usually only quotations need full sentences).
    - Add the required references, also called sources, within your speech, not just at the end.
- Consider using one or more presentational aids that do not use a screen, such as drawing on the board, holding up a book or other object, or audience participation.

List a non-screen-based aid suitable for your topic.

Tips for presentational aids:
1. Use the most interesting, unusual, but clear aids for your topic,
    a. Avoid using animals and children; they can be unpredictable.
    b. If you will use a screen, use mostly images, captions, quotes and statistics displayed as graphs. Don't allow the words on the screen to steal attention from the words you are saying and don't read your speech from the screen.
    c. If you project words on a screen, use large, simple font with strong color contrast from the background.
2. Make the visual available to all the audience simultaneously; avoid passing objects through the audience.
3. Hold or point to the visual when you talk about it; explain every aid you use.
    a. Thicker foam poster boards are more reliable than the thinner versions.
    b. You may use an assistant with models and real objects.

> Is there something that would be helpful for you to demonstrate or to have your audience try?

4. Check your electronics inside the venue where you will present. Also check the electronics that the venue supplies. Our classroom is generally available at lunch time.
5. Prepare a back-up plan for all presentational aids.
6. Practice with the visuals in a mirror or before family, friends or a recorder that you can play back to see how much the aid helps or distracts and to plan how to most effectively move with the aid.

Name the one best aid you could realistically prepare to clarify and reinforce your message.

Practice in appropriate attire with a timer.

General rules for how to dress for public speaking:
- Dress one level above the way that the audience will be dressed.
    - A third piece such as a sweater, jacket, vest, tie, or scarf lends a professional look.
    - Large accessories may distract.
- Wear clothes that you know you look great in.
    - Wear them for several hours on a day before you present to avoid surprises.
- Some topics are best presented in clothing that is not "professional" but appropriate to the topic.
    - Consider the shoes, clothing and accessories that would be most appropriate for you, your topic, audience, and occasion.
- Can you guess why it's important to practice in the outfit that you intend to wear on speech day?

> Shoes that are most appropriate for you, your topic, audience, and occasion:
>
> _____
>
> Clothing that is most appropriate for you, your topic, audience, and occasion:
>
> _____

Practice aloud 3 times with the "Oral Presentation Critique" p. ―――――.
Gain muscle memory for
- making eye contact
- pronouncing the words
- handling the visuals
- responding to feedback

Check the Confident chapter for controlling anxiety and for effective verbal and nonverbal messages.

> What makes you nervous about this speech?
>
> What can you do about it?
> What mental image will help?

Summarize the comments of your practice audience(s).

_____

On Your Presentation Day

Arrive and set up before class begins.
- Allow time for wait for the other presenters to set up as well.
  - Electronics?
  - Audience arrangement?
  - Lighting?
  - Practice with the person who will introduce you?
- Give an oral critique form to a friendly evaluator.
- Ask a friend to turn the time cards for you.
- Ask another friend to record you on your phone.

Bring 3 things.
- Video recording equipment (phone, laptop, tablet, etc.)
- Presentation aids
- Two Oral Presentation Critiques p._____for one for faculty and one for a peer.

Project confidence.
Avoid apologizing before you begin your speech or saying "thank you" at the end.
- Before your first word, take a second to plant your feet and look at the audience.
- After your last word, take a second to plant your feet and look at the audience.
  - Wait for the applause.
  - Gather materials and return to your seat.

After Your Presentation
- Enjoy the applause.
- Watch your video.
- Congratulate yourself.
- Reflect using either the
  - "Reflection of the Informative Speech p. _____
  - "Reflection of the Persuasive Speech p. _____

Informative Speech Outline Grading

Staple to front of your outline to avoid a 5 pt. penalty.

Title:	Brief (1), original (1), attention-getting (1) suggests, but does not reveal subject (2)	/ 5
Specific Speech Purpose:	Concise, specific, singular (2), audience-centered (2), aligned with main points (1)	/ 5
INTRODUCTION:	*Paragraph form:* Captures attention and interest (4) Establishes a friendly rapport and the credibility of the speaker (4) Previews the speech by listing the main points (4). Labels correctly each of the three parts: **(Attn) (Rap&Cred) (Prev)** (3)	/ 15

TRANSITIONS:	Summarizes previous point and/or introduces upcoming point
	    From the introduction to first main point (1)
	    Into each successive main point and the conclusion (4)
		/ 5

BODY OUTLINE:	Organizational pattern is appropriately <u>labeled</u> and implemented (5).
	
	 2-5 main points and all first-division sub-points use <u>parallel</u> (6)
	    <u>s</u>imple, <u>declarative</u> sentences, vivid, concise, and concrete,
	    fallacy-free, relating to the audience and the specific speech purpose. (10).
	
	 Each main point is developed with 2-5 sub-points, at least 3 supporting
	 materials with labels:
	    (explanation) (illustration) (statistics) (examples) (comparison)
	    (ex<u>pe</u>rt) (definition) and required **(visual <u>aids)</u>**. (15)
	
	 2-5 sub-points and sub-sub-points are supportive of the preceding
	    heading <u>indented</u> to group ideas
	    numbered/lettered correctly
	    with a <u>minimum of two</u> ideas per
	    grouping with only <u>one idea</u> per
	    outline point (5)
	
	 Typed single-sided according to this rubric and the workbook sample with
	    correct grammar, spelling, and punctuation (4)
		/ 45

CONCLUSION:	*Paragraph form:* Summarizes each main idea, adds no new ideas (5) Finishes with a short, easily memorize-able, powerful closing (5).	/ 10

Sources:	4 primary, recent, relevant, unbiased, credible references, including one interview (8)
	    APA form + qualification of the interviewee (2)
	    5 interview questions: open and informed (5)
		/ 15

Subtotal_____

-10 points per day LATE PENALTY _____

Section_____Name_____Grade_____

Oral presentations will be made **ONLY** after <u>acceptable outlines </u>have been submitted according to
    the schedule. Oral presentations are required to pass the course.
More than an average of 3 errors per page or 3 errors on page one = 0%.

Informative Speech Outline Sample

Branding the U.S.A.

SPECIFIC SPEECH PURPOSE: To help my audience understand the history of the flag of the United States.

INTRODUCTION:

When I was eight years old and even cuter than I am right now (Project a photo of me at age 8), my grandfather took me to a reenactment of the Civil War. The cannons, horses, and soldiers were big, loud, and spectacular enough to mesmerize the crowd; but they didn't mesmerize me. I was fixated on the flag. I thought it was wrong. It didn't have all the stars and stripes! No one else seemed concerned, which concerned me even more. I paid very little attention to the rest of the pageant. **(attention: anecdote) (credibility and rapport)** But the day was not a total waste. That day I began to learn how the United States flag has evolved from the time of North American exploration, colonial rule, revolution, and nationhood **(preview).**

TRANSITION:

I went back to the very beginning of America's history, a time when explorers first discovered and settled the North American continent.

BODY: (The Organizational Pattern Used is Chronological)

I. North Americans and explorers used flags for identity.
   A. Native American tribes displayed their totems and insignias.
   B. The Vikings displayed their personal flags.
      1. They sailed along the North American coast.
      2. The flag was white. **(Expert (Interview): Short)**
      3. The flag contained a black raven. **(visual of flag)**
   C. European explorers displayed their national flags.
      1. Christopher Columbus carried flags of Spain. **(Expert (Interview): Gilderlehrman)**
         a. National flag of Spain **(visual of flag)**
         b. Royal flag of Ferdinand & Isabella **(visual of flag)**
      2. John Cabot carried the flag of England. **(visual of flag)**
      3. Jacques Cartier carried the flag of France. **(visual of flag)**
      4. Henry Hudson carried the flag of the Netherlands. **(visual of flag)**
      5. Peter Minuit carried the flag of Sweden. **(visual of flag)**

TRANSITION:

The explorers eventually changed the coast into an organized set of English colonies and the flags changed.

II. Colonists used flags for unity with the British.
   A. The British King's Colors displayed Britain's control.
      1. The flag reminded colonists of **(visual of flag)** their British heritage.
      2. The flag reminded colonists of the British system of monarchy still in place.
         a. contained cross of St. George

b. contained cross of St. Andrew **(comparison)**

B. The British Red Ensign further displayed Britain's control.
1. The flag had a red background. **(visual of flag)**
2. The flag had the King's Colors in its canton.

TRANSITION:

But colonists began to resent Britain's control and they began creating their own flags rivaling the British banner.

III. Revolutionists used flags for opposition against the British.
A. Pine tree flags showed resentment in the northern colonies.
1. The pine tree was a local symbol. **(visual of flag)**
2. The pine tree was a popular village meeting place. **(Expert: Kupperman)**
B. Rattlesnake flags showed resentment in the southern colonies.
1. The rattlesnake was a symbol of vigilance. **(visual of flag)**
2. The rattlesnake was a symbol of deadly striking power.
3. The rattlesnake was a symbol of the union of the colonies.
a. some had 13 rattles **(explanation)**
b. one rattle was quiet alone, but a group was very loud **(comparison)**

TRANSITION:

Since flags of the Revolutionary Period had been mostly limited to symbolize particular regions, colonists realized they needed a national flag that contained something for everyone.

IV. Nationals used flags for their new country.
A. The Grand Union flag was the first U.S. national banner.
1. Commodore Esek Hopkins used the flag as the naval ensign. **(visual of flag)**
2. General George Washington used the flag as the standard of the Continental Army.
3. The Continental Congress used the flag as its proud emblem.
a. It was never officially approved
b. It was never formally recognized
B. The Stars & Stripes flag was the first "official" U.S. banner.
1. Congress passed a legal resolution concerning the design of an official national flag **(visual of flag)**
a. colors of red, white, and blue
(1) Red symbolized the blood shed to gain freedom
(2) White symbolized purity
(3) Blue symbolized courage and valor
b. 13 stars and 13 stripes to represent the 13 colonies
2. Congress never passed a legal resolution concerning recognition of the original designer of the flag.
a. many myths developed **(illustration of myths)**
b. Controversy continues today

        3. Congress passed another flag resolution dictating the method of representing new U.S. states on the flag.
            a. The 13 original stripes would always remain
            b. A new star would be added for each new state

TRANSITION:

With the addition of each new state to the Union, the U.S. flag has continued transforming.

CONCLUSION:

The changes in our flag reflect the changes in our nation from exploration to colonization, revolution, and growth **(summary).** When Grandpa and I drive by a U.S. flag, we see more than just a bold banner. We see one nation under God, indivisible striving for liberty and justice for all. **(clincher)**

References

Include the interview source after the other alphabetical, APA formatted sources.

    Ex. Doe, John. Personal interview. February 23, 2018. Gilcrease Museum Tour Guide.

Below the references, type 5 interview questions. See the example of the references and questions on the Persuasive Speech Outline Sample p._____.

Oral Presentation Critique

Speaker_____ Section_____

Title/Topic_____ Date _____

Grading: **5**=excellent **4**= very good **3**=good **2**=could be improvement **1**= needs improvement **0**=not observed

- Columns represent WPA Outcomes: 1. Aud. Analysis 2. Logical Organization 3. Style 4. Responsible Content

	1	2	3	4
I. INTRODUCTION 20%				
A. Dress & Hair: clean & appropriate for the topic and occasion				
B. First Words: captured audience attention and generated interest in topic				
C. Rapport & Credibility: established with audience verbally and non-verbally				
D. Preview of Specific Main Points: clear and obvious, including any necessary background				
II. BODY				
A. **Main Points** 10%				
1. Pattern: arranged logically, fallacy-free, consistent with professor's instruction				
2. Transitions between Main Points: summarized the previous main point specifically and obviously				
B. **Support** 20%				
Counts 1. Support: at least 3 varied supports for each main point, Definition_____ Twice Illustration_____ Statistic_____ Comparison_____ Example_____ Expert_____ Explanation_____				
2. Documentation for at Least Two Supports: Clearly cited visually and audibly				
3. Visual or Other Aids: clear & simple, clarified, supplemented, and boosted interest without distracting				
III. CONCLUSION 15%				
A. Summary: named each one of the main points obviously and specifically				
B. New Information: gave no new information in the conclusion				
C. Final Words: short, clever sentence or phrase summarized entire speech (not "Thank you" or "That's it")				
IV. DELIVERY 25%				
A. Speaking: fluent, extemporaneous, conversational, appropriate pronunciation and grammar				
B. Posture, Movement, & Gestures: natural and effective, handled visuals efficiently				
C. Eye Contact with the Audience: 80% - 90% of the time, equal among all sections				
D. Vocalics: articulate, well-modulated rate, pitch, and projection, few fillers _____				
E. Facial Expressions: complimented the message and mood				
V. EFFECT 10%				
A. Content & Wording: Ideas were new & tailored for this audience, concise, parallel, & concrete.				
B. Either Informative: Avoided persuasive messages: "should", "ought", "must", "do", don't"				
Or Persuasive: Question & Answer: paraphrased questions, finished w/ a summary/clincher				

Main points &/or other notes:

I.

II.   Total points _____   **%**

III.   1 point deduction for every 15 seconds short or long _____

IV.   **Informative**: 4 - 5 minutes

(V).   **Persuasive**: 6 - 8 minutes before the 2 minute Q & A period

Professors: for the persuasive speech only, enter the four WPA scores into d2l" under **COMMUNICATION SKILLS** Revised **4A 1911**. Average each column/outcome & convert to a 4 point scale (x 0.8). Students: submit nothing.	4	7	5	4

Evaluator_____ Duration _____

Oral Presentation Critique Speaker_____Section_____

Oral Presentation Critique

Speaker_____ Section_____

Title/Topic_____ Date _____

Grading: 5=excellent 4= very good 3=good 2=could be improvement 1= needs improvement 0=not observed

- Columns represent WPA Outcomes: 1. Aud. Analysis 2. Logical Organization 3. Style 4. Responsible Content

	1	2	3	4
I. INTRODUCTION 20%				
A. Dress & Hair: clean & appropriate for the topic and occasion				
B. First Words: captured audience attention and generated interest in topic				
C. Rapport & Credibility: established with audience verbally and non-verbally				
D. Preview of Specific Main Points: clear and obvious, including any necessary background				
II. BODY				
A. **Main Points** 10%				
1. Pattern: arranged logically, fallacy-free, consistent with professor's instruction				
2. Transitions between Main Points: summarized the previous main point specifically and obviously				
B. **Support** 20%				
Counts 1. Support: at least 3 varied supports for each main point, Definition_____ Twice Illustration _____ Statistic _____ Comparison_____ Example _____ Expert _____ Explanation_____				
2. Documentation for at Least Two Supports: Clearly cited visually and audibly				
3. Visual or Other Aids: clear & simple, clarified, supplemented, and boosted interest without distracting				
III. CONCLUSION 15%				
A. Summary: named each one of the main points obviously and specifically				
B. New Information: gave no new information in the conclusion				
C. Final Words: short, clever sentence or phrase summarized entire speech (not "Thank you" or "That's it")				
IV. DELIVERY 25%				
A. Speaking: fluent, extemporaneous, conversational, appropriate pronunciation and grammar				
B. Posture, Movement, & Gestures: natural and effective, handled visuals efficiently				
C. Eye Contact with the Audience: 80% - 90% of the time, equal among all sections				
D. Vocalics: articulate, well-modulated rate, pitch, and projection, few fillers _____				
E. Facial Expressions: complimented the message and mood				
V. EFFECT 10%				
A. Content & Wording: Ideas were new & tailored for this audience, concise, parallel, & concrete.				
B. Either Informative: Avoided persuasive messages: "should", "ought", "must", "do", don't"				
Or Persuasive: Question & Answer: paraphrased questions, finished w/ a summary/clincher				

Main points &/or other notes:

I.

II.   Total points _____   **%**

III.   1 point deduction for every 15 seconds short or long _____

IV.   **Informative**: 4 - 5 minutes

(V).   **Persuasive**: 6 - 8 minutes before the 2 minute Q & A period

Professors: for the persuasive speech only, enter the four WPA scores into d2l" under **COMMUNICATION SKILLS** Revised **4A 1911**. Average each column/outcome & convert to a 4 point scale (x 0.8). Students: submit nothing.	4	7	5	4

Evaluator_____ Duration _____

Oral Presentation Critique   Speaker_____Section_____

Reflection of the Informative Oral Presentation

This is one of the 4 reflections that comprise the 200 point "Reflections Grade".

Purpose: To synthesize information, solve problems, and clarify your values.

Procedure: View the recording of your speech at least twice. Type a 3 paragraph essay. Some professors require this page stapled on top of the essay and submitted to dropbox.

1. The first of 3 paragraphs is about current successes.
   - Include descriptions of 3 specific examples from the recording that show your development of 3 different skills for which you can feel proud of so far.
   - Include a label for each of the 3 skills.
     - Highlight each label in color. Gray is a color.
     - Use vocabulary words from the textbook or items from the workbook's grading sheets for the labels.   /10

2. The second of the 3 paragraphs is about future improvement.
   - Include a description of 1 specific example from the recording that shows an area that you'd like to target for personal growth before your next presentation.
   - Include a label for this growth area.
     - Highlight the label in color. Gray is a color.
     - Use a vocabulary word from the textbook or an item from the workbook's grading sheets for the label.   /10

3. The third of the 3 paragraphs is about your plan to improve upon either a strength or a weakness.
   - Include one or more simple, specific, observable actions that you can realistically see yourself accomplishing, actions which over time can generate improvement in your targeted skill.
     - Include the days, weeks, and/or times that you can realistically accomplish these actions.
     - Highlight the WHEN words in color.   /20

4. Details:
   - **Title:** Use two lines to title your document "Reflection of the Oral Presentation of the Informative Speech" on line one, and your speech title on line two.
     Example: Reflection of the Oral Presentation of the Informative Speech
     "Don't Look Down!"
   - **Length:** Use at least one whole page and no more than two pages.
   - **Concluding, single sentence:** Obviously state the one most important thing you are learning about public speaking.   /10

Total_____/50 points   _____100%

Student name_____Section_____Date due: _____

See example on next page.

More than an average of 3 errors per page or more than 3 errors on page one = 0%

Student's Name_____
Instructor's Name_____
COM 101 Section #_____
Date____

Reflection of the Oral Presentation of the Informative Speech
"The 'Why' Generation"

For my informative speech, I presented on the topic of Generation Z and faith. I have been passionate about this topic for several years and did extensive research on it for my high school senior project. As a part of that project, I had to present in front of judges and my peers in a public school. Now presenting at a Christian university, my presentation style had to be altered to meet the needs of a new audience. During my presentation in class, I was proud of my extemporaneous and conversational speaking that not only addressed the content but was also tailored to my unique audience that, unlike my previous audience, already understood the value of an identity in Christ. My gestures and movement added to this natural conversation-style presentation through complementary hand motions and visual usage. I also impressed the audience with my ability to emphasize and transition between my main points by confidently walking from one side of the screen to the other.

Although my body language projected confidence, at certain moments during the presentation, I sounded out of breath. This indicated that I was struggling with some nerves and was speaking too quickly. This lack of proper breathing led to occasional vocalic lapses, such as poor articulation, overly quick rate, and the usage of fillers.

For my next presentation, I will improve my vocalics by breathing steadily, speaking slower, and enunciating my words. During my informative speech, I spoke too quickly because I was trying to present too much information in a relatively short amount of time. When I am creating my persuasive speech outline, I will condense and organize my research to maximize the 6-8 minutes while also allowing time to pause and emphasize important information. I will note the supporting facts that I could remove if I end up struggling to effectively fit the content into the time frame. Throughout the week leading up to my persuasive speech, I will practice breathing properly before and during my presentation. I will record myself to note my rate and enunciation and then adjust accordingly with each succeeding run-through. In preparation for my informative presentation in Oral Communication, I learned the important public-speaking skill of condensing extensive research while maintaining its effectiveness and connection to the audience.

Please see instructions on the previous page.

Persuasive Speech Outline Grading

Staple to front of your outline to avoid a 5pt. penalty

Title:	Brief (1) original (1) attention-getting (1) suggests, but does not reveal the subject (2)	/ 5
Proposition of:	(Fact, Value, or Policy) audience centered, correctly labeled, specifically worded (5)	/ 5

INTRODUCTION:	*Paragraph form:* Captures attention and interest (4)
	    Establishes a friendly rapport and the credibility of the speaker (4)
	    Previews the speech by listing the main points (4)
	    Labels correctly each of the three parts: **(Attn) (Rap&Cred) (Prev)** (3)
		/ 15

TRANSITIONS:	Summarizes previous point and/or introduces upcoming point
	    From the introduction to first main point (1)
	    Into each successive main point and the conclusion (4)
		/ 5

BODY OUTLINE:	Organizational pattern is appropriately <u>labeled</u> and implemented (5).
	
	2-5 main points and/or first-division sub-points are <u>parallel</u> (6)
	(Monroes requires parallelism for Capital letters, but not for Roman Numerals.)
	    simple, <u>declarative</u> sentences, vivid, concise, and concrete, fallacy-free
	    relating to the audience and proposition. (10).
	
	Each main point is developed with 2-5 sub-points, at least 3 supporting materials
	with labels:
	    (explanation) (illustration) (statistics) (examples) (comparison) (expert)
	    (definition) and required **(visual aids)** (15)
	
	2-5 sub-points and sub-sub-points are supportive of the preceding heading
	    <u>indented</u> to group ideas
	    numbered/lettered correctly
	    with a <u>minimum of two</u> ideas per grouping with only <u>one idea</u> per line (5)
	
	Typed single-sided according to this rubric and the workbook sample with
	    correct grammar, spelling, and punctuation (4)
		/ 45

CONCLUSION:	*Paragraph form:* Summarizes each main idea, adds no new ideas (5) Finishes with a short, easily memorize-able final statement/powerful closing (5).	/ 10

SOURCES:	4 primary, recent, relevant, unbiased references, including one interview (8)
	    APA form + qualification of the interviewee (2) (See outline sample)
	    5 interview questions: open and informed (5)
		/ 15

Subtotal_____

-10 points per day LATE PENALTY = _____

Section _____ **Name** _____ **Grade** _____

Oral presentations will be made **ONLY** <u>after acceptable outlines</u> have been submitted according to
    the schedule. Oral presentations are required to pass this course.
More than an average of 3 errors per page or 3 errors on page one = 0%.

Persuasion

Three major differences between the informative and persuasive speaking are
- The "Specific Speech Purpose" vs. the "Proposition"
- The organizational patterns
- The question and answer period

Just after the title, the informative speech outline assignment asked for a "Specific Speech Purpose" while the persuasive asks for a "Proposition of fact, value, or policy".

A proposition of <u>fact</u> asserts that something is true or false.
Ex. Global warming is caused by humans.

A proposition of <u>value</u> asserts that something is good or bad.
Ex. Disposable diapers harm the environment.

A proposition of <u>policy</u> has "should", "ought", or "must". Policy calls the audience to action.
Ex. ORU's Board of Trustees should form a committee to raise support for a football program.

Any proposition, whether fact, value, or policy is specific and positive.

Word the Proposition

Topic: Tobacco

☹ *vague* - Growing tobacco should be illegal.

☹ *negative* - Tobacco should not be grown here.

☺ *Specific and positive* – You and I should actively support the current bill prohibiting the production and sale of tobacco in the United States.

Label each Proposition: FACT...VALUE...or...POLICY (Ask your professors for the answers.)

1.____Cigarette smoking is the most prevalent use of addictive drugs in America today.

2.____The tobacco moguls have lied to the American public concerning the safety of cigarette smoking.

3.____The tobacco industry's leaders should be prosecuted for misleading America's cigarette smoking population.

4.____The tobacco industry is guilty of the murder of millions of Americans.

5.____It is unfair that tobacco farmers get rich at the expense of addicting teens to a life destined to end in death by lung cancer.

6.___The manufacturers of cigarettes should be required to reimburse the health care systems for the care of lung cancer patients.

7.___Growing tobacco is an immoral and sinful occupation.

8.___Criminalizing the growing of tobacco and the manufacture and sale of tobacco products would cause a major, negative economic impact upon the state of Alabama.

9.___The State of Oklahoma should make the sale of all tobacco products to persons under 25 years of age a felony punishable by a minimum of 10 years imprisonment.

10.___A Christian cannot be involved in any phase of the tobacco industry without breaking the Ten Commandments.

Use the Appropriate Organizational Pattern.

Some professors require propositions of policy and this adaptation of Monroe's Motivated Sequence.

I.   (NEED) Explain the problem with no hint that there is a solution. Avoid the word, "need" because the words that follow "need" will be the solution which you must conceal until the SATISFACTION step. Use logos and pathos. Spend ½ of the total speech time on the problem. Make your audience feel wrong, angry or scared so that they almost beg you for an answer.

II.   (SATISFACTION) Describe the organizations, institutions, businesses or governments that are helping to solve the problem.

III.   (VISUALIZATION OF THE FUTURE) Paint a word picture of a likely, future situation appropriate to the members of this audience. Describe that future situation if we do nothing, or if we work to solve the problem, or both. Use no present or past tense. Only future tense.

IV.   (CALL TO ACTION) Use Arabic numerals to list 3-5 baby steps toward the solution: observable, varied, and effective. Start each baby-step with a verb. Tailor the steps for individuals in your audience to start and complete within a few minutes or a few days.

Questions and Answers

Conduct a Q & A session immediately after your 6-8 minute persuasive presentation.
- Clarify ideas.
- Refute arguments immediately and gently.
- Involve and engage the audience.

Plan ahead, keep control, and finish strong.
- Plant a few questions before the speech that you are well-prepared to answer to encourage hesitant audience members.
- Hold the microphone.
  - Recognize and complement the questioner.
  - Paraphrase the question.
- Respond to the entire audience, not just the questioner.
  - Keep answers brief, relate back to specific points in the speech.
  - Ask if you answered adequately if you're interested in further engagement with that questioner.
- Conclude by repeating your main points, perhaps offering to continue discussion later, and either the same or a different clincher.

Write three questions to plant before your persuasive speech.

- Tear this page into three parts for three different audience members.
- Choose audience members who will sound and look authentic and natural.
- Call on your "plants" **only if** authentic questions are not available.

_____

_____

Questioner: Please practice asking this question **aloud** before the speech. Raise your hand when the Q&A begins.

_____

_____

Questioner: Please practice asking this question **aloud** before the speech. Raise your hand when the Q&A begins.

_____

_____

Questioner: Please practice asking this question **aloud** before the speech. Raise your hand when the Q&A begins.

Persuasive Speech Outline Sample

A Waste of Time

PROPOSITION OF POLICY: Students who want to keep the world clean should live cleaner lives.

INTRODUCTION:
A few months ago, I went on a prayer walk through my neighborhood. I live way out of the way, close to the woods in Colorado. So, a prayer walk for me consists of walking through the woods to pray. As I walked one day, I noticed something that bothered me. Trash. Trash all over the place. Almost every major fast food company was represented and most major grocery stores in the area. This surprised me. I was 10 miles out of town! No one comes out to my area, yet there was so much trash!!! **(Attention: anecdote)** But this isn't a problem in just my hometown, this is a problem in everyone's hometown. **(Credibility and Rapport)** The world is experiencing a trash crisis but I have found several steps that we can take as students to pass on a healthier, cleaner planet. **(Preview).**

TRANSITION: Before we discuss these steps, what exactly are we facing?

BODY: (The Organizational Pattern Used is the Monroe's Motivated Sequence)

I.   (NEED): Waste is a global problem.

      A.   Poorer nations are drowning in trash.

          1.   Guatemala City trash homes. **(examples)**

          2.   Pakistan dumps. (visuals)

      B.   Larger nations are oblivious.

          1.   Americans produce about 7 lbs. a day. **(statistics)** according to...

          2.   The USA produces around 220 million tons. **(statistics)**

      C.   The oceans are becoming garbage dumps.

          1.   5.25 trillion pieces of trash in the ocean **(statistics)**

    2.   Harms wildlife.

    3.   Breaks down to mircoplastics,

        a. travels through food chain.

        b. https://www.youtube.com/watch?v=Yu5Dw6rwZvE **(examples)**

    4.   Doesn't completely break down.

TRANSITION: Even though this looks daunting, we can still overcome it.

    II.   (SATISFACTION): Individuals and groups are organized to help.

        A.   Keep America Beautiful develops public, private, and civic partnerships to create a clean, green, and beautiful America.

            1.   KAB.org sponsors events to end littering and improve recycling. **(visual of website)**

            2.   KAB.org sponsors events to beautify main streets. **(visual of the event)**

        B.   OKRA, Oklahoma Recycling Association, is a non-profit organization established to improve the business of recycling.

            1.   OKRA provides education and referral services.

            2.   OKRA promotes reduction, reuse, recycling, and composting.

            3.   OKRA serves as a central communication point for exchange among businesses. **(visual of website)**

TRANSITION: Every state in the union has an organization you and I can partner with to overcome the trash crisis, but what would happen if we don't get involved, if we wait until we're older or if we let someone else get involved?

    III.   (VISUALIZATION OF THE FUTURE): Doing nothing will ruin our future.

     A.   The amount of trash will become impossible to overcome.

         1.   Trash produced increases annually. **(statistics from U.S. Environmental Protection Agency)**

            a. Micro plastics will add to the risks of local flooding by clogging drains. **(quote Andrady 2017)**

            b. Flooding from clogged drains will be more prevalent inside individual homes.

            c. Flooding from sinks and toilets onto floors and carpets and into neighboring apartments will become common.

         2.   Flooding odors often remain long after the water has drained.

     B.   The amount of trash will kill most wildlife.

         1.   Animals consume trash and die. **(example)**

         2.   Trash inhibits seedlings from growing **(example)**

TRANSITION: The future is grim but we can change it.

    IV.   (CALL TO ACTION): Global cleanliness starts with you.

     A.   Take small steps.

         1.   Keep your room clean. **(explanation)**

         2.   Pick up after yourself and don't assume others will do it.

     B.   Take considerate steps.

         1.   Walk trails with trash bags ready. **(examples)**

         2.   Recycle. **(examples)**

         3.   Commit a crime and join a chain gang to clean sides of highways.

TRANSITION: Start with these small steps of consideration; you can save the world.

CONCLUSION:

Although we are nearly drowning in our own trash, both national and state organizations have already begun cleaning our world. If we don't join them or take our own initiative, our children may be deprived of beautiful landscapes, clean air to breathe and water to drink. By living clean lives and cleaning up after others, we will take our planet back. Help me. Help each other. Start by cleaning your room, making your bed, recycling, and cleaning up after others. Together, we can make a difference. I promise you, this will not be a waste of you time.

Works Cited

Brown, Caleb. Interview. 17 November 2016. (Clean room fanatic. Has maintained a clean room for ten years)

Kaplan, Sarah. "By 2050, there will be more plastic than fish in the world's oceans, study says." The Washington Post, Web. 20 January 2016

Moore, Charles J. "Choking the Oceans with Plastic" The New York Times, Web. 14 August 2014

Parker, Laura. "Ocean Trash: 5.25 Trillion Pieces and Counting, but Big Questions Remain." National Geographic, Web. 11 January 2015

United States Congress, "Advancing Sustainable Materials Management: Facts and Figures." *Advancing sustainable Materials Management: Facts and Figures,* EPA, 19 Jan. 2017. www.epa.gov/smm/advancing-sustainable-materials-management-facts-and-figures.

Interview primary, open, informed questions:

1. Why do you strive to keep your room clean?

2. What steps do you take to ensure that you maintain your room's cleanliness?

3. What are the pros and cons of a clean room in your opinion?

4. How has a clean room helped you in your daily life?

5. How highly would you recommend this lifestyle to others?

Oral Presentation Critique

Speaker_____ Section_____

Title/Topic_____ Date _____

Grading: **5**=excellent **4**= very good **3**=good **2**=could be improvement **1**= needs improvement **0**=not observed

- Columns represent WPA Outcomes: 1. Aud. Analysis 2. Logical Organization 3. Style 4. Responsible Content

	1	2	3	4
I. INTRODUCTION 20%				
A. Dress & Hair: clean & appropriate for the topic and occasion				
B. First Words: captured audience attention and generated interest in topic				
C. Rapport & Credibility: established with audience verbally and non-verbally				
D. Preview of Specific Main Points: clear and obvious, including any necessary background				
II. BODY				
A. Main Points 10%				
1. Pattern: arranged logically, fallacy-free, consistent with professor's instruction				
2. Transitions between Main Points: summarized the previous main point specifically and obviously				
B. Support 20%				
Counts 1. Support: at least 3 varied supports for each main point, Definition_____ Twice Illustration_____ Statistic_____ Comparison_____ Example_____ Expert_____ Explanation_____				
2. Documentation for at Least Two Supports: Clearly cited visually and audibly				
3. Visual or Other Aids: clear & simple, clarified, supplemented, and boosted interest without distracting				
III. CONCLUSION 15%				
A. Summary: named each one of the main points obviously and specifically				
B. New Information: gave no new information in the conclusion				
C. Final Words: short, clever sentence or phrase summarized entire speech (not "Thank you" or "That's it")				
IV. DELIVERY 25%				
A. Speaking: fluent, extemporaneous, conversational, appropriate pronunciation and grammar				
B. Posture, Movement, & Gestures: natural and effective, handled visuals efficiently				
C. Eye Contact with the Audience: 80% - 90% of the time, equal among all sections				
D. Vocalics: articulate, well-modulated rate, pitch, and projection, few fillers _____				
E. Facial Expressions: complimented the message and mood				
V. EFFECT 10%				
A. Content & Wording: Ideas were new & tailored for this audience, concise, parallel, & concrete.				
B. Either Informative: Avoided persuasive messages: "should", "ought", "must", "do", don't"				
Or Persuasive: Question & Answer: paraphrased questions, finished w/ a summary/clincher				

Main points &/or other notes:		%
I.		
II.	Total points _____	
III.	1 point deduction for every 15 seconds short or long _____	
IV.	**Informative**: 4 - 5 minutes	
(V).	**Persuasive**: 6 - 8 minutes before the 2 minute Q & A period	

Professors: for the persuasive speech only, enter the four WPA scores into d2l" under **COMMUNICATION SKILLS** Revised **4A 1911**. Average each column/outcome & convert to a 4 point scale (x 0.8). Students: submit nothing.	4	7	5	4

Evaluator_____ Duration _____

Oral Presentation Critique Speaker_____Section_____

Oral Presentation Critique

Speaker_____ Section_____

Title/Topic_____ Date _____

Grading: **5**=excellent **4**= very good **3**=good **2**=could be improvement **1**= needs improvement **0**=not observed

- Columns represent WPA Outcomes: 1. Aud. Analysis 2. Logical Organization 3. Style 4. Responsible Content

	1	2	3	4
I. INTRODUCTION 20%				
A. Dress & Hair: clean & appropriate for the topic and occasion				
B. First Words: captured audience attention and generated interest in topic				
C. Rapport & Credibility: established with audience verbally and non-verbally				
D. Preview of Specific Main Points: clear and obvious, including any necessary background				
II. BODY				
A. **Main Points** 10%				
1. Pattern: arranged logically, fallacy-free, consistent with professor's instruction				
2. Transitions between Main Points: summarized the previous main point specifically and obviously				
B. **Support** 20%				
Counts 1. Support: at least 3 varied supports for each main point, Definition_____ Twice Illustration _____ Statistic _____ Comparison_____ Example _____ Expert _____ Explanation_____				
2. Documentation for at Least Two Supports: Clearly cited visually and audibly				
3. Visual or Other Aids: clear & simple, clarified, supplemented, and boosted interest without distracting				
III. CONCLUSION 15%				
A. Summary: named each one of the main points obviously and specifically				
B. New Information: gave no new information in the conclusion				
C. Final Words: short, clever sentence or phrase summarized entire speech (not "Thank you" or "That's it")				
IV. DELIVERY 25%				
A. Speaking: fluent, extemporaneous, conversational, appropriate pronunciation and grammar				
B. Posture, Movement, & Gestures: natural and effective, handled visuals efficiently				
C. Eye Contact with the Audience: 80% - 90% of the time, equal among all sections				
D. Vocalics: articulate, well-modulated rate, pitch, and projection, few fillers _____				
E. Facial Expressions: complimented the message and mood				
V. EFFECT 10%				
A. Content & Wording: Ideas were new & tailored for this audience, concise, parallel, & concrete.				
B. Either Informative: Avoided persuasive messages: "should", "ought", "must", "do", don't"				
Or Persuasive: Question & Answer: paraphrased questions, finished w/ a summary/clincher				

Main points &/or other notes:

I.

II.   Total points _____   **%**

III.   1 point deduction for every 15 seconds short or long _____

IV.   **Informative**: 4 - 5 minutes

(V).   **Persuasive**: 6 - 8 minutes before the 2 minute Q & A period

Professors: for the persuasive speech only, enter the four WPA scores into d2l" under **COMMUNICATION SKILLS** Revised **4A 1911.** Average each column/outcome & convert to a 4 point scale (x 0.8). Students: submit nothing.	4	7	5	4

Evaluator_____ Duration _____

Oral Presentation Critique   Speaker_____Section_____

Reflection of the Persuasive Oral Presentation

This is one of the 4 reflections that comprise the 200 point "Reflections Grade".

Purpose: To synthesize information, solve problems, and clarify your values.

Procedure: View the recording of your speech at least twice. Type a 4 paragraph essay. Some professors require this page stapled on top of the essay and submitted to the dropbox.

1. The first of 4 paragraphs is about current successes.
   - Include descriptions of 3 specific examples from the recording that show your development of 3 different skills for which you can feel proud.
   - Include a label for each of the 3 skills.
      - Highlight each label in color. Gray is a color.
      - Use vocabulary words from the textbook or items from the workbook's grading sheets for the labels.   /10

2. The second of the 4 paragraphs is about future improvement.
   - Include a description of 1 or more specific example(s) from the recording that shows an area that you'd like to target for personal growth before your next presentation.
   - Include a label for this growth area.
      - Highlight the label in color. Gray is a color.
      - Use a vocabulary word from the textbook or an item from the workbook's grading sheets for the label.   /10

3. The third of the 4 paragraphs is about your plan to improve upon either a strength or a weakness.
   - Include one or more simple, specific, observable actions that you can realistically see yourself accomplishing, actions which over time or immediately can generate improvement in your targeted skill.
      - Include the days, weeks, and/or times that you can realistically accomplish these actions.   /10
      - Highlight the WHEN words in color.

4. The fourth of the 4 paragraphs is about the level of success you had with the action plan you wrote in the reflection of your informative speech.
   - Include the parts of your plan that worked well, if any and the parts that didn't work well, if any.
   - Explain why you think that the successful parts of your plan were successful and why you think that the unsuccessful parts of your plan were unsuccessful.   /10

5. Details:
   - **Title:** Use two lines to title your document "Reflection of the Oral Presentation of the Persuasive Speech" on line one, and your speech title on line two.
     Example: Reflection of the Oral Presentation of the Informative Speech "Saving Lives Three Times a Day"
   - **Length:** Use at least one whole page and no more than two pages.
   - **Concluding, single sentence:** Obviously state the one most important thing you are learning about public speaking.   /10

Total_____/50 points   _____100%

Student name_____Section_____Date due: _____

See example on next page.

More than an average of 3 errors per page or more than 3 errors on page one = 0%

Student's Name_____
Instructor's Name_____
COM 101 Section #_____
Date____

Reflection of the Oral Presentation of the Persuasive Speech
"Design Detective"

Giving this speech was uncharted territory for me, I was uncertain about presenting in a persuasive style. However, by utilizing the resources available to me and preparing adequately, I rose to the occasion and delivered a quality persuasive speech. The strongest aspect of my presentation was my vocalics. I spoke clearly, articulating my words and projecting the necessary amount for the size of the audience in the room. There were few to no fillers, and my confident yet conversational tone conveyed the message well. My tone, in addition to the usage of anecdotes, established rapport and credibility. I told stories about my life that related to the audience and my topic. Knowing that my audience would be my Christian peers, I compiled content and wording tailored to them. Lofty scientific and philosophical concepts are challenging to grasp and engage with, so I carefully selected my supporting elements and planned how I would explain them in an understandable and applicable way.

Although my main points were interesting and consistent with Monroe's Motivated Sequence, the portion on "Visualization of the Future" was slightly underdeveloped. This section somewhat blended in with the "Satisfaction" portion. I did not make the word picture of a typical future situation clear. My slide title, "Future Expert Engagement," made the "future" point clear, but neither my words nor any other visual helped my audience to imagine themselves in a hypothetical future situation. The "Action" section lacked a relative timeline, which could have left audience members confused about the steps needing to be addressed.

The next time I give a speech, especially when I need to condense a lot of information into a short amount of time, I will make sure that my main points are apparent not only visually but also verbally. When I am creating the outline, I will write the main points and their supports detailed and consistent with the pattern chosen. If I decide to use Monroe's Motivated Sequence again, I will develop realistic scenarios in the "Visualization" section on the outline. In the week leading up to my speech, I will practice incorporating the relevant details and emphasizing each main point. I will check that my visual aids support the content delivered and prompt me, as necessary.

During my previous informative speech, my main area for improvement was my vocalics. I tried to condense too much information into a short period and did not breathe properly before and during my presentation. In my reflection on that speech, I said that I would condense the information as necessary and practice breathing to prevent poor articulation, an overly fast rate, and the usage of fillers. Although I did not take every step that I had outlined in the reflection, I did look over it during my persuasive speech preparation. I practiced my presentation multiple times, using a stopwatch to make sure that I stayed in the 6-to-8-minute range. When I went significantly over time, I cut out unnecessary information. I also made sure that I was taking deep breaths before and during my practice speeches and the real deal. Therefore, my improvement action plan was successful; it increased my awareness of vocal preparation and led to observable growth during my persuasive speech. As a result of taking Oral Communication, the most important thing that I have learned about public speaking is that it is not as intimidating as it seems – it is simply an informed conversation with a group of people about a relevant topic.

Please see instructions on the previous page.

Final Exam Study Guide

Final Exam Study Guide

The exam questions are drawn from the vocabulary of each chapter and appendix as well as the objectives listed below. The level of exam questions range from identification of definitions to application of principles. As the exams change each semester, this study guide is not a definitive list of all the objectives that will be on the exam. Instead this guide is a list of the objectives that have often been represented on previous final exams.

Chapter	Objectives
1	B, E, K, L
2	B, C, F, G, H, I, J
3	E, G
4	B, C, D, F, G
5	C, E, F, G, H, J
6	C, E, J, M, N
7	B, D, E
8	C, D, E, H, I, L
9	C, D, G, I, J
10	B, H, I, J, N, O, P, R
11	C, D, F
12	B, C, E, G, H
13	B, E, J, K, P, Q
14	G, J, K, M, N
15	G, H, J, K
APPENDIX A	A
APPENDIX B	A
APPENDIX C	C, E, F
APPENDIX D	D, E

"You gain strength, courage and confidence by every experience
in which you really stop to look fear in the face…
You must do the thing you think you cannot do."

—Eleanor Roosevelt

"Let no one despise you for your youth, but set the believers an example in speech, in conduct, in love, in faith, in purity."

—The Apostle Paul. I Timothy 4:12^{ESV}